NEGOTIATING OIL AND GAS LEASES:

A Book for Land Owners

Mike May, P.E.

www. Negotiating Oil and Gas Leases .com

Negotiating Oil and Gas Leases:

A Book For Land Owners

Copyright © 2012 by Mike May, P.E.

All rights reserved.

Mike May, P.E.

(832) 382 - 9976

mike.may @ limestoneoil .com

www. Negotiating Oil and Gas Leases .com

Investors Publishing

www.investorspublishing.com

ISBN-13: 978 - 061 543 74 84

This book is dedicated to

Acknowledgements:

I would like to acknowledge all of the efforts and the fortitude of the mineral rights owners across America who do faithfully receive their oil and gas royalty checks month after month and year after year, some by mail and some by direct deposit, and who do deposit those sums time after time in to their weary old bank accounts without ever a cross word or a long face.

God Bless America!!!

Contents

Chapter 2

Goals and Strategies When Negotiating an Oil and Gas Lease. . . 15

Chapter 3

Oil & Gas Leases Clause-by-Clause 43

Chapter 4

Questions to Ask Before You Sign an Oil and Gas Lease 113

Chapter 1

Introduction and Definitions

I wrote this book to help Land Owners and Mineral Rights Owners like you negotiate Oil and Gas Leases with oil companies. Perhaps you have already been approached by oil companies who want to lease your land to drill oil or natural gas wells on your property and you want to make the most of it.

Nice things can happen! The opportunity to lease your land for oil and natural gas exploration is one of the greatest economic opportunities of your lifetime. Where else can you simply sign one piece of paper (an Oil and Gas Lease) – do nothing else ever – and potentially receive millions of dollars or tens of millions of dollars in production royalties? Nowhere! With so much at stake you want to get the terms in the Oil and Gas Lease right and this book was written to help you. We'll start with a few pertinent definitions.

Then we will discuss your goals and your strategies for achieving your goals when negotiating an Oil and Gas Lease. You want to make as much money as possible while giving the oil companies everything they need to accomplish this purpose but nothing more.

You may be approached by different kinds of oil companies from time to time. Their methods of operating as well as their intentions vary. You need to understand the differences between the various oil companies and you need to have a unique strategy for negotiating with each kind of Oil Company. Few land owners understand this.

Next we will go through the terms and clauses of an Oil and Gas Lease in great detail so that you understand the important negotiating points in an Oil and Gas Lease.

Then I will provide you with 14 Questions You Should Ask Before You Sign an Oil and Gas Lease.

Let's get started with some definitions!

Definitions in Oil and Gas Law

Oil and Gas Lease - An Oil and Gas Lease is a written contract wherein a mineral interest owner, known as the Lessor, grants the right to explore for oil, natural gas, and other hydrocarbons for a specific period of time to an oil company or other entity, known as the Lessee. An Oil and Gas Lease is both a conveyance and a contract. It conveys certain mineral rights and establishes conditions which the Lessee must meet during the term of the lease.

Mineral Interest - A mineral interest in oil and gas is the right to search for, develop, and produce oil and gas on a tract of land and the right to possess oil and gas in place under a property. In most nations of the world, the government owns all of the mineral rights. However, the United States is an exception. In the U.S. most of the mineral rights are privately owned. Although the federal and state governments do own the mineral rights under federal and state lands.

Mineral Interest Implied Easement Ownership of the mineral interest in a tract of land includes not only ownership of the minerals but also an implied easement to use the surface as is reasonably necessary to extract the minerals. Without this implied easement, a mineral interest would be worthless.

Mineral Interest Incidents - In addition to the right to search for, develop, and produce oil and gas, a mineral interest also includes the following four incidents:

a. The right to receive profits from, and the obligation to pay the costs incurred in, developing minerals.

b. The right to sell the mineral interest.

c. The right to lease a mineral interest to another person or entity through an oil and gas lease. The right to lease is referred to as the executive right when it is severed from the rest of the mineral interest.

d. The right to benefits provided under the terms of an Oil and Gas Lease. These benefits include a royalty, delay rentals, shut-in royalty payments, and a lease bonus.

Surface Interest - The surface interest is all of the other interests in a property that are not included in the mineral interest. The surface interest is encumbered by and servient to the mineral interest.

Sovereignty - In the beginning all land was owned by the government. This time period is known as sovereignty. Individual land ownership in the United States began when governments first granted lands to private citizens and companies. Afterward, ownership was passed forward from one person or entity to another by deed or other conveyance through to the present day.

Severability - The first private ownership after sovereignty included both surface rights and mineral interests. Many land tracts today are owned by individuals who still retain both the surface rights and the mineral interests. However, surface rights and mineral rights are severable. That means that they can be conveyed separately. The result is that one person or entity may own the surface interest in a tract of land while another person or entity may own the mineral interest.

Leasehold Interest - A leasehold interest is the right to the mineral interest that is conveyed by a Lessor to a Lessee through an oil and gas lease. A leasehold interest is also called a working interest. This is the interest that is possessed by an oil company that has leased a property for oil and gas exploration.

Royalty Interest - A royalty interest is a share of the revenue received from production. A land owner's royalty or Lessor's royalty is the share of production revenue stated in the royalty clause of an oil and gas lease. If a successful well is drilled, this royalty represents the bulk of the financial reward the mineral interest owner will receive in return for leasing their mineral interest to a Lessee. Royalty interest owners do not have any surface use rights that stem from their royalty interest.

Overriding Royalty Interest (ORRI)
An overriding royalty is a royalty granted by a leasehold interest owner by filing a simple assignment of such an interest in the public records. Overriding royalties are usually granted as compensation to Geologists, Geophysicists, Land Men, Attorneys, and others who contribute time and professional services to a drilling venture. An overriding royalty terminates when the underlying Oil and Gas Lease terminates.

Enforceability of a Contract - A contract is a legally enforceable promise between two or more parties to do or not to do a particular thing.

Certain items must be present to create a contract:

a. An offer.

b. Acceptance of the offer without qualification.

c. Sufficient consideration.

d. Legal subject matter.

e. Competent parties.

f. Intent of the parties to enter into a contract.

An Oil and Gas Lease only needs to be signed by the Lessor (the Mineral Interest Owner). Recording of the Oil and Gas Lease in the county courthouse by the Lessee implies acceptance of the Lease by the Lessee.

Definitions of Terms in
Oil and Gas Leases

Royalty - A royalty is a share of the proceeds from the sale of oil and gas produced from a petroleum property.

Primary Term - The primary term is the period of time designated in the habendum clause (term clause) in most Oil and Gas Leases during which an Operator is granted the right to begin drilling operations without the obligation to do so. Most Oil and Gas Leases state that the lease shall be in force for a primary term of a specific number of years - typically one to five years - from the date that the lease is executed (signed), and for as long thereafter as oil or gas or other substances are produced in paying quantities from the leased premises or from lands pooled or unitized therewith. If the lease is not producing in paying quantities and the Operator is not engaged in continuous drilling operations at the end of the primary term, then the Oil and Gas Lease usually terminates.

Lease Bonus - A lease bonus is a sum of money paid by the Lessee (Oil Company) to a Lessor (Mineral Interest Owner) as an incentive and as good and valuable consideration at the time an Oil and Gas Lease is executed (signed) by a Lessor. The amount is negotiable and is often based on a certain number of dollars per acre of land being leased.

Delay Rental - A delay rental is a payment made by the Lessee (Oil Company) to the Lessor (Mineral Rights Owner) in an Oil and Gas Lease that extends the primary term of the lease and thus extends the time that the Lessee has available to begin drilling on the lease premises. A "Paid Up Lease" is an Oil and Gas Lease that does not include provisions for Delay Rentals. In a "Paid Up Lease" the primary term is set at the time the lease is executed and no delay rental payments are ever required.

Note: There are many more oil and gas definitions in the glossary of this book if you need them.

Chapter 2

Goals and Strategies When
Negotiating an Oil and Gas Lease

Nowhere else can you simply sign one piece of paper - an Oil and Gas Lease – and potentially receive millions of dollars in production royalties. Your sole goal is to make as much money as possible while giving the oil companies everything they need to accomplish this purpose but nothing more. For you as a Land Owner, the most important terms in an Oil and Gas Lease are: the royalty, the primary term length, the lease bonus, and the delay rentals.

Two Kinds of Oil Companies

You will generally be approached by one of two different kinds of oil companies. Each of these two different kinds of oil companies has different plans. Let's talk about each of them.

1. Do-Nothing-For-the-Next-Several-Years Oil Companies

Advantage: These companies tend to pay higher lease bonuses.

Disadvantage: They usually will not drill any wells on your property for several years after you sign the lease - if they ever drill any wells at all.

2. Drill-or-Shoot-Seismic-In-12-Months-Or-Less Oil Companies

Advantage: These companies take action in less than 12 months so you may start receiving royalty checks very soon.

Disadvantage: They pay modest lease bonuses. But you may not mind this because most of the money that you may potentially receive through an Oil and Gas Lease is from royalties – not from the lease bonus. And they may not require a long primary term. A primary term as short as 12 months may suffice.

Both of these two kinds of oil companies can be good oil companies but their methods and their immediate intentions are different. First, let's discuss the Do-Nothing-For-the-Next-Several-Years Oil Companies.

Do-Nothing-For-the-Next-Several-Years Oil Companies

These are usually very large oil companies that engage in very large projects involving tens of thousands of acres of land. You will never see a large oil company lease just 40 acres of land and drill just one well. They just don't do that. Large oil companies tend to lease many thousands of acres of land (perhaps 10,000 to 100,000+ acres of land per project) which will include your land and most or all of your neighbors' lands. Their modus operandi is to establish control of a very large amount of contiguous acreage and then develop it intelligently by first performing geological studies and geophysical surveys over the whole area and then drilling dozens, hundreds, or even thousands of wells. This endeavor takes many years to complete so the odds of you seeing any immediate seismic surveying activity or the drilling of wells on your land is unlikely because your land is only a small part of a much larger project. Thus we call these companies the Do-Nothing-For-the-Next-Several-Years Oil Companies. The advantage in leasing to them is that they tend to pay higher lease bonuses. The disadvantage is that it takes years for them to shoot seismic and drill wells on your property if they ever do it at all. So any potential royalty from production will be delayed or non-existent.

Not Picky in the Beginning

When Do-Nothing-For-the-Next-Several-Years Oil Companies are in the initial phase of leasing land they are not picky. They will attempt to lease virtually all land within a wide swath on a map. They do this by employing Land Men who are employees of their company as well as independent contract Land Men who together approach as many mineral interest owners as they can find and ask them to sign long-term Oil and Gas Leases so that they can quickly obtain control over as much acreage as possible. Sometimes they are able to quietly lease all of the acreage within an area before anyone else becomes aware of what they are doing. On other occasions word of their efforts will leak out and another group of actors called Land Speculators will appear.

Land Speculators

Land Speculators are also Do-Nothing-For-the-Next-Several-Years Companies but they are not really oil companies. They are more precisely Do-Nothing-For-the-Next-Several-Years-NON-Oil-Companies because their business model does not include producing oil. When Land Speculators hear that a large oil company is trying to lease all of the land in a particular area they will move at high speed to try to lease tracts of land in that area before the large oil company can get to them. The Land Speculators are hoping that they will be able to lease your land from you and later sell (assign) their position in the lease to a larger oil company so that the larger oil company can fill in the gaps of land that they missed in their effort to

20

lease everything everywhere.

Land Speculators are not concerned about producing oil and gas. They have no intention of doing so. They have no Petroleum Engineers, few if any Geologists, shoot no seismic, and drill no wells. They are only interested in buying and selling acreage. Incredible as it may sound, Land Speculators are often not concerned with whether or not a tract of land holds potentially good locations to drill oil and gas wells. Their battle cry is "Who cares if it's a good place to drill or not? It's acreage!" This is a risky proposition because a large oil company will become more picky toward the end of the leasing phase. As lease bonus rates rise ever higher toward the end of the leasing phase the large oil company's in-house Land Men will consult their Geologists more and more to decide which tracts of land they really need and which ones they can live without. In the end, the large oil company may never purchase the Land Speculators' leases. If that is the case the Land Speculator will generally experience massive financial loss. And if you leased to one of these Land Speculators you will be dead in the water until the Oil and Gas Lease expires because Land Speculators do not shoot seismic and they do not drill wells.

The only good point about a Land Speculator is that they may offer you a high lease bonus (a lot of money) to sign a lease. But you must understand that they have no intention of drilling any wells on your land. If you lease to a Land Speculator, you will have to wait until the Land Speculator sells (assigns) your lease to a true oil company and that oil company takes action in the field before you have a chance to receive royalties from production. This could take years.

How to Tell the Difference

Of course you won't know a Land Speculator from a real Oil Company by their name. None of them have the words "Land Speculators" on their business cards. They all have names that sound like oil companies and talk a good game. The only way you can tell the difference is by asking a lot of questions and by examining the lease terms they require!

Land Speculators will almost never consider a lease or a seismic permit with action required in the field in 12 months or less because they need time to find a buyer; and that buyer will require that there be many years remaining in the primary term of the lease.

The Herd Mentality

Whenever and wherever large oil companies are leasing large amounts of land there tends to be a herd mentality and a rush of the crowd to lease every parcel of land in the area. The crowd includes herd-following oil companies and land speculators. Perhaps 60% of the population are trend followers and herd followers at heart. Similarly perhaps 60% of the oil and gas industry's leasing activity is involved in herd-following at all times. Herd followers perceive the areas they are in as scarce productive areas. These apparent scarce but productive areas are easy to spot. They are the plays on the covers of magazines, the subject of television segments, and the focus of newspaper articles. They even receive attention from local politicians. If your land is located in one of these hot areas where there is a lot of activity, you can sit back and lease your land to the highest frenzied bidder. Just don't wait until the end when Lessee's start to come to their senses. The highest lease bonuses are being paid when about 70% of the available land has been leased.

It's OK to lease your land to these kinds of companies as long as you understand what you are doing. It will take years to shoot seismic over the entire area (your land and the surrounding 50,000 to 100,000+ acres), interpret all of the data, and drill wells over the entire area. So it will be a long time before you receive any production royalty checks – if ever.

As an alternative, you might offer to grant a true oil company a 12-18 month seismic permit for a modest sum which would allow them to include your property in a massive seismic shoot of the area. By doing this you will insure that any drilling prospects on your property will be identified in the seismic data. But rather than granting a 3-year or 5-year Oil and Gas Lease at the outset you might grant an option to execute a 3-year or 5-year Oil and Gas Lease at any time during the 12-18 months that the seismic permit is in effect. If you do this, the oil company will probably only execute the 3-year or 5-year Oil and Gas

Lease if they see something promising on seismic. And if not, your property will be free again in 12-18 months rather than in three to five years.

Drill-or-Shoot-Seismic-In-12-Months-Or-Less Oil Companies

The second kind of Oil Company is the Drill-or-Shoot-Seismic-In-12-Months-Or-Less Oil Company. These are often small and mid-size companies that are ignoring the herd. They don't care where the crowd is working. In fact, they may be actively avoiding the crowd. They may approach you in a quiet area. Drill-or-Shoot-Seismic-In-12-Months-Or-Less Oil Companies are true oil companies. They are usually leasing a smaller area (perhaps 40 acres to 5,000 acres) and they are trying to drill their first well relatively soon. They may or may not shoot seismic before they drill the first well. They have shorter timelines than the larger oil companies and the land speculators. Your lease is probably a much more important part of their total project than it is to a larger company that is leasing the whole countryside. Small and mid-size companies will not offer high bonuses; but they can take action. The offering of a company willing to make substantial investments in your property through either seismic or drilling of wells must be seriously considered because it could lead to you receiving production royalty checks – and soon. This is the most economically beneficial outcome for you from any Oil and Gas Lease!

In summary some companies may offer you a high lease bonus and will control your land without drilling or shooting seismic for many years - if ever. You will get a large lease bonus up front but you may never get any royalty. Meanwhile, other companies may offer a modest lease bonus but be willing to take action and invest large amounts of money in seismic and/or drilling very soon – say within 6-12 months. This second group of companies is far more likely to actually drill wells on your land and provide you with the opportunity to earn the inordinate sums of cash that come from production royalties.

How do I know what kind of Oil Company I'm dealing with and how do I negotiate with any given company?

By now you should be asking, "How do I know what kind of Oil Company I'm dealing with and how do I negotiate with any given company?" Fortunately, you can make an offer that works well for either type of Oil Company. And you can assess what kind of company they are by the terms that they insist on.

First consider this: Large Do-Nothing-For-the-Next-Several-Years Oil Companies that are leasing large swaths of the countryside and the Land Speculators they have in tow must have long-term leases! Always! Their business plan will not work with short-term leases. They must have a long primary term or an option to extend the primary term and thus control your land for many years. They know this and they will be willing to pay higher bonuses and higher delay rentals as a result. But Drill-or-Shoot-Seismic-In-12-Months-Or-Less Oil Companies will be willing to at least discuss shorter term arrangements especially if you offer lower lease bonuses in return for shorter term leases.

Strategy for Do-Nothing-For-the-Next-Several-Years Companies

Your strategy when dealing with Do-Nothing-For-the-Next-Several-Years Companies which includes Land Speculators is simple: Get as much money as you can up front because that may be all of the money you ever get. You are giving up control of your land for many years so get as much money as possible in return. This will be in the form of a high lease bonus and possibly high delay rentals that will be paid to you annually for several years.

In any given area there is a range of possible royalties. With these kinds of companies you can ask for a royalty at the high end of the range and get it because Do-Nothing-For-the-Next-Several-Years Oil Companies have a lot of money and they are in a frantic hurry to lease land regardless of whether or not what they are doing makes economic sense for them. Remember, they are operating in a feeding frenzy of sorts.

Strategy for Drill-or-Shoot-Seismic-In-12-Months-Or-Less Oil Companies

In contrast, Drill-or-Shoot-Seismic-In-12-Months-Or-Less Oil Companies do not need long-term leases. That is not to say they won't ask for one. They will. But they don't need nearly as much time as the larger companies or the Land Speculators. These companies are not in a feeding frenzy. They tend to be reserved, careful, thoughtful, and methodical. And because they are not following the herd they do not need to lease your land – but they would like to. A sound approach is to find out what the company has in mind and then help them get what they need. Recognize that the larger the project in terms of land area, the more time they may require for development. A 5,000 acre project will take more time to fully develop than a 160-acre square. Keep this in mind. Talk through the development process step by step and well by well. If the oil company does not feel that they will have enough time to drill all of the wells that they may want to drill after investing great sums in a seismic shoot, they will walk away. So be reasonable.

Drill-or-Shoot-Seismic-In-12-Months-

Or-Less Oil Companies are willing to make substantial investments in your land within the next twelve months. They are proposing a course of action that may yield the highest possible economic benefit for you: royalties from producing oil and gas wells. They are offering you an extremely rare and exciting opportunity. Help them. They will offer a modest lease bonus and a reasonable royalty. The royalty may be dependent on the length of the primary term and the size of the lease bonus. They may pay a slightly higher royalty if you give them a break on the lease bonus.

If you are in a quiet area you may not have had any other offers for several years and there may not be any more offers for several more years if you do not reach an agreement with these people. Ask them what they want to do. Ask them how much time they need. Consider going forward initially in baby steps that allow them to gradually increase their commitments and their investments over time while having the option to stop at any time. If they are willing to either shoot seismic or drill a well within twelve months then you should make it easy for them to do so.

An Offer to Go Forward in Baby Steps

Here's an offer that might work for both of you. You could grant them a 12-month seismic permit with an Option to execute an Oil and Gas Lease any time during the 12 months that the seismic permit is in effect. You might grant the seismic permit for a modest $5 to $15 per acre while simultaneously agreeing that the lease bonus for the Oil and Gas Lease will be $50 per acre and will cover only the first year if they choose to execute the Option to lease. The Oil and Gas Lease could have a three-year primary term with say $75 delay rentals due at the beginning of the second and third years.

Under an arrangement like this the Drill-or-Shoot-Seismic-In-12-Months-Or-Less Oil Company can start shooting seismic and performing geologic research with only a small up-front cost which is the $5 to $15 per acre for the seismic permit. Having an Option to Lease in hand they will find it easy to enlist a partner if they wish. They will only pay the higher $50/acre lease bonus if they see something exciting on the seismic survey or if they otherwise want to drill a well for any reason. They must exercise their option to execute an Oil and Gas Lease and they must pay you the $50/acre lease bonus before they can drill the first well. And they will only have to pay you the $75/acre annual delay rentals if they elect to hold your land for a second or third year under the lease without drilling a well. This will cost them additional money but it will give them the comfort of knowing that they will have more than enough time to drill all of the drilling locations they identify on the seismic survey in the event of some unexpected delay. It's great for you because you will either get a well drilled soon or you will get a lot of money in lease bonus and delay rentals. They will find this arrangement attractive. And it is fair for you because they will have to pay you more money if they hold your land for a longer-than-expected time.

Make Finding Partners & Capital Easy

Drill-or-Shoot-Seismic-In-12-Months-Or-Less Oil Companies may also need to find partners or raise capital. Oil companies that have a signed Oil and Gas Lease in their hand (signed by you), have a much easier time finding partners and raising capital within the oil and gas industry than those who simply have great ideas. This holds true even when the leases they have in hand are only short-term leases or seismic permits with options to lease. Capital owners love to act on signed leases and just roll their eyes at great ideas. Help your guy raise drilling capital by placing at least a short-term signed lease in his hand.

12 Months is Plenty of Time

The twelve months granted in the seismic permit is plenty of time to decide whether or not to exercise the Option to execute an Oil and Gas Lease. Some companies will offer you a short-term drilling commitment as part of a longer-term lease. This may be an attractive offer for you. The company proposes an Oil and Gas Lease with a long primary term - say 3 to 5 years - but they also commit to drilling the first well within a short period of time – say 12 months. If they do not drill the first well within that short period of time – the lease terminates and you are again in control of your land and you are ready for the next opportunity. If they do drill a well within the specified short period of time they will have "earned" the long-term lease which they will then be operating under and they will have ample time to drill additional wells. You are agreeing to a long-term lease but you are assured of getting at least one well drilled in the first twelve months or getting you land back – a fair bargain.

Seismic

Shooting seismic is a good thing. Often after performing a seismic survey an oil company will identify locations where they would like to drill wells. If so, they can exercise their Option to execute an Oil and Gas Lease and pay you the $50 per acre lease bonus to cover the first 12 months of the primary term. If they take this step they will almost certainly drill at least one well. This is what can bring you hundreds of thousands and even millions of dollars in royalties. If they do not identify any drilling locations and they do not want to drill any wells then the Seismic Permit with an Option to Lease will expire after 12 months. You will have pocketed the seismic permit money and you will again be in complete control of your land and ready for the next opportunity.

If the company insists on a long term lease – say three to five years – and they will not give you a commitment to either shoot seismic or drill a well soon; then you know you are dealing with a Do-Nothing-For-the-Next-Several-Years Company. If this is the case, insist on a high lease bonus, high delay rentals, and a royalty at the high end of the range if you do anything at all.

Royalty

Remember that the royalty is where most of your money will be made. You must be reasonable but there is no reason to compromise below a fair royalty regardless of whether you are working with a large company or a small company or with a long-term lease or a short-term lease.

A fair royalty will be lower in a quiet area and higher in a hot area. Most areas of the U.S. are quiet. If you are in a feeding-frenzy area you will know it because you will be receiving multiple offers to lease your land each month. If you are in a quiet area, you will know it because you will receive few if any offers within a year's time. Make it easy for someone to come in and get started. If your terms are too tough they will have difficulty when they attempt to raise capital or find partners for your project and you will unknowingly harm your chances of having your land developed. Easier up-front terms in the Seismic Permit and Lease Option and in the Oil and Gas Lease will make it easier for your Lessee to find partners, raise capital, and get moving!

Once you get something started the momentum builds and the project goes forward without any further effort on your part. Just never compromise on a reasonable royalty. That's where the money is.

Now that we have an understanding of some of the matters involved in a lease negotiation, let's discuss the terms of an Oil and Gas Lease in detail clause-by-clause.

Chapter 3

Oil and Gas Leases Clause-by-Clause

Before drilling a well an oil company must acquire the rights to drill for and produce oil and natural gas on a tract of land. The necessary document is and Oil and Gas Lease. An Oil and Gas Lease is a written contract wherein a mineral interest owner, known as the Lessor, grants the right to explore for oil, natural gas, and other hydrocarbons to an oil company or other entity, known as the Lessee, for a specific period of time. Before we discuss how mineral interests are conveyed, let's discuss what a mineral interest is.

Mineral Interest

A mineral interest in oil and gas is the right to search for, develop, and produce oil and gas on a tract of land and the right to possess oil and gas in place under a property. In most nations of the world, the government owns all of the mineral rights. However, the United States is an exception. In the U.S. most of the mineral rights are privately owned, although the federal and state governments do own a substantial portion of the total mineral rights because they own the mineral rights under federal and state lands.

Mineral Interest Implied Easement

Ownership of the mineral interest in a parcel of land includes not only ownership of the minerals but also an implied easement to use the surface as is reasonably necessary to extract the minerals. Without this implied easement, a mineral interest would be worthless.

Mineral Interest Incidents

In addition to the right to search for, develop, and produce oil and gas, a mineral interest also includes the following four incidents:

The right to receive profits from and the obligation to pay costs incurred in a search to develop minerals.

The right to sell the mineral interest.

The right to lease a mineral interest to another person or entity through an oil and gas lease. The right to lease is referred to as the executive right when it is severed from the rest of the mineral interest.

The right to benefits provided under

the terms of an oil and gas lease. These benefits include a royalty, delay rentals, shut-in royalty payments, and a lease bonus.

Surface Interest

The surface interest is all other interests in a property that are not included in the mineral interest. The surface interest is encumbered by and servient to the mineral interest.

Sovereignty

In the beginning, all land was owned by the government. This time period is known as sovereignty. Individual land ownership in the United States began when governments first granted lands to private citizens. Ownership was passed forward from one person to another by deed, by inheritance, or by other conveyance through the present day.

Severability

The original ownership after sovereignty included both surface rights and mineral interests. Many land tracts today are owned by an individual who still retains both the surface rights and the mineral interests. However, surface rights and mineral rights are severable. That means that they can be conveyed separately. The result is that one person or entity may own the surface interest in a tract of land while another person or entity may own the mineral interest.

Leasehold Interest

A leasehold interest is the right to the mineral interest that is conveyed by a Lessor to a Lessee through an oil and gas lease. A leasehold interest is also called a working interest. This is the interest that is possessed by an oil company that has leased a property for oil and gas exploration.

Royalty Interest

A royalty interest is a share of the revenue received from production. A land owner's royalty or Lessor's royalty is the share of production revenue set out in the royalty clause of an oil and gas lease. If a successful well is drilled, this royalty represents the bulk of the financial reward the mineral interest owner will receive in return for leasing their mineral interest to a Lessee. Royalty interest owners do not have any surface use rights that stem from their royalty interest.

Overriding Royalty Interest

An overriding royalty is a royalty granted by a leasehold interest owner by filing a simple assignment of such in the public records. Overriding royalties are usually granted as compensation to Geologists, Geophysicists, Land Men, Attorneys, Investment Sponsors and others who contribute time and professional services to a drilling venture. An overriding royalty terminates when the underlying oil and gas lease terminates.

Oil and Gas Leases

An oil and gas lease is a written contract wherein a mineral interest owner, known as the Lessor, grants the right to explore for oil, natural gas, and other hydrocarbons for a specific period of time to an oil company or other entity, known as the Lessee. An oil and gas lease is both a conveyance and a contract. It conveys certain mineral rights and establishes conditions which the Lessee must meet during the term of the lease.

An oil and gas lease is considered a "Deed with the Possibility of Reverter" which means the interest may revert to the Lessor when the lease expires.

Enforceability of a Contract

A contract is a legally enforceable promise between two or more parties to do or not to do a particular thing.

Certain items must be present to create a contract:

- An offer.

- Acceptance of the offer without qualification.

- Good and valuable consideration.

- Legal subject matter.

- Competent parties.

- Intent of the parties to enter into a contract.

An oil and gas lease need only be signed by the Lessor. Recording of the oil and gas lease in the county courthouse by the Lessee implies acceptance of the Lease by the Lessee.

Case Law and Modern Lease Language

Oil and gas leases have existed for decades. When the industry was in its infancy, oil and gas leases were simpler and often silent on many key points. But in the fullness of time, numerous civil cases have been adjudicated to yield an abundance of case law. Modern oil and gas leases are written with the advantage of having decades of industry activity and thousands of pages of oil and gas case law. So modern oil and gas leases have language that covers most of the eventualities that are encountered.

Key Clauses in Oil and Gas Leases

The following are key clauses that are included in most oil and gas leases:

Granting Clause

The granting clause of an oil and gas lease describes the land area that is covered by the lease, what substances are covered by the lease – such as oil and gas and other minerals, and what rights are being acquired by the Lessee. The terms "gas" may also be further defined to include or not include any gaseous substance – not just hydrocarbon gases. For example, helium is a valuable product that may be produced. It is a gaseous substance but it is not a hydrocarbon so clarity is required.

Example Granting Clause

In consideration of a cash bonus in hand paid and the covenants herein contained, Lessor hereby grants, leases and lets exclusively to Lessee the following described land, hereinafter called leased premises:

(Legal Description Inserted Here)

In the County of _____,

In the State of _____,

Containing _____ross acres, more or less, including any interests which Lessor may hereafter acquire by reversion, prescription or otherwise), for the purpose of exploring for, developing, producing and marketing oil and gas, along with all hydrocarbon and non-hydrocarbon substances produced in association therewith ("Oil and Gas Substances"). The term "gas" as used herein includes helium, carbon dioxide, gaseous sulfur compounds, methane produced from coal formations and other commercial gases, as well as normal hydrocarbon gases.

Mother Hubbard Clause

A "Mother Hubbard" clause of an oil and gas lease is often included in the granting clause. It acts to include all land owned by the Lessor, if any, that are adjacent to and contiguous with the land in the legal description so that the lease covers all land owned by the Lessor in that location, regardless of whether the legal description perfectly describes the boundaries of the land. In this way, no small slivers of land are inadvertently left out of the lease.

Example Mother Hubbard Clause

In addition to the above-described land, this lease and the term "leased premises" also covers accretions and any small strips or parcels of land now or hereafter owned by Lessor which are contiguous or adjacent to the above-described land, and, in consideration of the aforementioned cash bonus, Lessor agrees to execute at Lessee's request any additional or supplemental instruments for a more complete or accurate description of the land so covered.

In Gross Provision

An In Gross provision in an oil and gas lease is also often included in the granting clause to establish the number of acres that a lease will be assumed to contain, regardless of whether it contains slightly more or less, so that payments in the lease that are based on the number of acres can be made with certainty even when the exact acreage of a lease may be unknown or later found to be slightly higher or lower than it was believed to be at the time a lease was signed.

Example In Gross Provision

For the purpose of determining the amount of any payments based on acreage hereunder, the number of gross acres above specified shall be deemed correct, whether actually more or less.

Term Clause (Also known as the Habendum Clause)

The term clause of an oil and gas lease, also known as the habendum clause, defines the duration of the lease. This is usually divided in to two parts: the primary term and the extended term. The primary term is essentially the amount of time that a Lessee has to drill the first well. Simply speaking, if the drilling of a well is not begun during the primary term, the lease expires. If at least one well is drilled during the primary term, then the extended term defines the amount of time that the lease will remain in effect -- usually for as long as a well produces in paying quantities.

Example Term Clause or Habendum Clause

This lease shall be in force for a primary term of 3 years from the date hereof, and for as long thereafter as oil or gas or other substances covered hereby are produced in paying quantities from the leased premises or from lands pooled or unitized therewith or this lease is otherwise maintained in effect pursuant to the provisions hereof.

Dry Hole & Cessation of Production Clauses

The dry hole and cessation of production clauses in an oil and gas lease describe how a lease will be maintained in the event that a dry hole is drilled or all production from an existing well ceases.

Example Dry Hole & Cessation of Production Clauses

If Lessee drills a well which is incapable of producing in paying quantities (hereinafter called "dry hole") on the

leased premises or lands pooled or
unitized therewith, or if all production
(whether or not in paying quantities)
permanently ceases from any cause,
including a revision of unit boundaries
pursuant to the provisions of this lease
or the action of any governmental
authority, then in the event this lease
is not otherwise being maintained
in force it shall nevertheless remain
in force if Lessee commences further
operations for reworking an existing
well or for drilling an additional well
or for otherwise obtaining or restoring
production on the leased premises or
lands pooled or unitized therewith
within 90 days after completion
of operations on such dry hole or
within 90 days after such cessation
of all production. If after the primary
term this lease is not otherwise being
maintained in force, but Lessee is then
engaged in Operations, as defined
below, this lease shall remain in force
so long as any one or more of such

Operations are prosecuted with no interruption of more than 90 consecutive days, and if any such Operations result in the production of Oil and Gas Substances, as long thereafter as there is production in paying quantities from the leased premises or lands pooled or unitized therewith. After completion of a well capable of producing in paying quantities hereunder, Lessee shall drill such additional wells on the leased premises or lands pooled or unitized therewith as a reasonably prudent operator would drill under the same or similar circumstances to (a) develop the leased premises as to reservoirs then capable of producing in paying quantities on the leased premises or lands pooled or unitized therewith, or (b) protect the leased premises from uncompensated drainage by any well or wells located on other lands not pooled or unitized therewith. There shall be no covenant to drill exploratory wells or any additional wells except as expressly provided herein. As used herein, the term Operations shall mean any activity conducted on or off the leased premises that is reasonably calculated to obtain or restore production, including without limitation, (i) drilling or any act preparatory to drilling (such as obtaining permits, surveying a drill site, staking a drill site, building roads, clearing a drill site, or hauling equipment or supplies); reworking, plugging back, deepening, treating, stimulating, refitting, installing any artificial lift or production-enhancement equipment or technique; constructing facilities related to the production, treatment, transportation and marketing of substances produced from the lease premises; (iv) contracting for marketing services and sale of Oil and

Gas Substances; and (v) construction of water disposal facilities and the physical movement of water produced from the leased premises.

Rental Clause

The rental clause of an oil and gas lease describes certain conditions that may be necessary to hold a lease in force during the primary term. If a lease is "paid-up" at the time it is signed, that means that no further payments are required by the Lessee to keep the lease in effect during the primary term. If a lease is not a "paid-up" lease, the Lessee is usually required to make annual delay-rental payments to the Lessor during the primary term if a well is not drilled. If so, the exact amount and place of payment are provided in the rental clause. The amount is often a fixed dollar amount and the place of payment is often a bank.

Some leases specify that if the Lessee makes a good faith error in paying the delay rental, such as the wrong dollar amount or to the wrong location, the Lessor must notify the Lessee and the Lessee has 30 days to correct the payment. This clause has been upheld in Texas, Kincaid v. Gulf Oil Corporation, (Texas Ct. App. 1984).

Example Rental Clause

If on or before the first anniversary date hereof operations for the drilling of a well for oil or gas or other substances covered hereby have not been commenced on the leased premises or lands pooled or unitized therewith, or if there is no production in paying quantities from the leased premises or lands pooled or unitized therewith, then subject to Paragraph this lease shall terminate as to both parties unless Lessee on or before that date pays or tenders to Lessor or to Lessor's credit at _____, or its successors, which shall be Lessor's depository agent for receiving payments regardless of changes in the ownership of said land, the sum of $_____ as rental covering the privilege of deferring the commencement of operations for the drilling of a well for a period of twelve months from said anniversary date. In like manner and upon like payments or tenders, the commencement of operations for the drilling of a well may be further deferred for one or more twelve-month periods during the primary term of this lease. All payments or tenders may be made in currency, or by check or by draft, and such payments or tenders to Lessor or to the depository by deposit in the U.S. Mails on or before the rental due date in a stamped envelope addressed to the depository or to the Lessor at the last address known to Lessee shall constitute proper payment. If the depository should liquidate or be succeeded by another institution, or for any reason fail or refuse to accept rental payment hereunder, Lessee shall not be held in default for failure to make such payment until 60 days after Lessor has delivered to Lessee a proper recordable instrument naming another institution as depository agent to receive payments. If on or before any rental due date Lessee in good faith makes an erroneous rental payment by paying the wrong person or the wrong depository or the wrong amount, Lessee shall be unconditionally obligated to pay or tender proper rental for the period involved and this lease shall continue in effect as though such rental payment had been properly made, provided that proper rental shall be paid or tendered within 30 days after receipt by Lessee of written notice of the error from Lessor, accompanied by any documents and other evidence necessary to enable Lessee to make proper payment. Lessee may pay or tender any rental at any time in advance of its due date to the Lessor then known to Lessee as provided in Paragraph _____ and such payment or tender shall bind all persons then or thereafter claiming any part of such rental.

Royalty Clause

The royalty clause of an oil and gas lease describes how the Mineral Interest owner's royalty will be calculated royalties are generally a fixed percentage of the net proceeds of product sales. But adjustments are often made for a Lessor's proportionate share of state and county taxes on the production. Modern royalty clauses often specify that the Lessor's royalty will be calculated from the actual revenue received from the sale of the product rather than the older term which based the royalty calculation on the "market value at the well" which was ambiguous. Generally royalties are free of the cost of bringing oil and gas from the reservoir to the surface. However, Lessors' royalties are often adjusted for their proportionate share of the cost, if any, of moving the product from the well site to the buyer and of any post-production activities such as treating, processing, or compression that is necessary to make the product marketable – regardless of whether those costs are incurred on or off of the lease premises. These clarifications in the royalty clause resulted from Texas Oil & Gas Corp. v. Vela, (Texas 1968) where an operator was selling gas under a long-term contract at a price that was less than the spot price other operators in the area were receiving for their gas, and from Wood v. TXO Production Corp., (Oklahoma 1992) where the cost of compression as a marketing process came under close scrutiny.

Example Royalty Clause

For all Oil and Gas Substances that are physically produced from the leased premises, or lands pooled, unitized or communitized therewith, and sold, Lessor shall receive as its royalty 18.75 % of the sales proceeds actually received by lessee or, if applicable, its affiliate, as a result of the first sale of the affected production to an unaffiliated party, less this same percentage share of all Post Production Costs and this same percentage share of all production, severance and ad valorem taxes. As used in this provision, Post Production Costs shall mean all costs actually incurred by lessee or its affiliate and all losses of produced volumes whether by use as fuel, line loss, flaring, venting or otherwise from and after the wellhead to the point of sale. These costs include without limitation, all costs of gathering, marketing, compression, dehydration, transportation, removal of liquid or gaseous substances or impurities from the affected production, and any other treatment or processing required by the first unaffiliated party who purchases the affected production. For royalty calculation purposes, lessee shall never be required to adjust the sales proceeds to account for the purchaser's costs or charges downstream of the point of sale.

Lessee or its affiliate shall have the

right to construct, maintain and operate any facilities providing some or all of the services identified as Post Production Costs. If this occurs, the actual costs of such facilities shall be included in the Post Production Costs as a per barrel or per mcf charge, as appropriate, calculated by spreading the construction, maintenance and operating costs for such facilities over the reasonably estimated total production volumes attributable to the well or wells using such facilities.

If Lessee uses the Oil and Gas Substances (other than as fuel in connection with the production and sale thereof) in lieu of receiving sale proceeds, the price to be used under this provision shall be based upon arm's-length sale(s) to unaffiliated parties for the applicable month that are obtainable, comparable in terms of quality and quantity, and in closest proximity to the leased premises. Such comparable arm's-length sales price shall be less any Post Production Costs applicable to the specific arms-length transaction that is utilized.

Shut-in Royalty Clause

A shut-in royalty clause of an oil and gas lease describes how payments may be made to a Lessor by a Lessee if a well is shut-in. Payment of shut-in royalties allows the Lessee to maintain the lease in full force as if the well were producing in paying quantities. A limiting clause may be included that limits the amount of time that a lease may be maintained by shut-in royalties.

Example Shut-In Royalty Clause

If after the primary term one or more wells on the leased premises or lands pooled or unitized therewith are capable of producing Oil and Gas Substances in paying quantities, but

such well or wells are either shut in
or production therefrom is not being
sold by Lessee, such well or wells shall
nevertheless be deemed to be producing
in paying quantities for the purpose of
maintaining this lease. If for a period of
90 consecutive days such well or wells
are shut in or production therefrom is
not sold by Lessee, then Lessee shall
pay an aggregate shut-in royalty of one
dollar per acre then covered by this
lease. The payment shall be made to
Lessor on or before the first anniversary
date of the lease following the end of
the 90day period and thereafter on
or before each anniversary while the
well or wells are shut in or production
therefrom is not being sold by Lessee;
provided that if this lease is otherwise
being maintained by operations under
this lease, or if production is being sold
by Lessee from another well or wells on
the leased premises or lands pooled or
unitized therewith, no shut-in royalty
shall be due until the first anniversary

date of the lease following the end of the 90day period after the end of the period next following the cessation of such operations or production, as the case may be. Lessee's failure to properly pay shut-in royalty shall render Lessee liable for the amount due, but shall not operate to terminate this lease.

Pooling Clause

A pooling clause in an oil and gas lease enables a Lessee to combine several leases in to a single one-well unit as may be required to meet the spacing requirements of the state oil and gas regulatory agency.

Example Pooling Clause

Lessee shall have the right but not the obligation to pool all or any part of the leased premises or interest therein with any other lands or interests, as to any or all depths or zones, and as to any or all substances covered by this lease, either before or after the commencement of drilling or production, whenever Lessee deems it necessary or proper to do so in order to prudently develop or operate the leased premises, whether or not similar pooling authority exists with respect to such other lands or interests. The creation of a unit by such pooling shall be based on the following criteria (hereinafter called "pooling criteria"): A unit for an oil well (other than a horizontal completion) shall not exceed 40 acres plus a maximum acreage tolerance of 10%, and for a gas well or a horizontal completion shall not exceed 640 acres plus a maximum acreage tolerance of 10%; provided that a larger unit may be formed for an oil well or gas well or horizontal completion to conform to any well spacing or density pattern that may be prescribed or permitted by any governmental authority having jurisdiction to do so. For the purpose of the foregoing, the terms "oil well" and "gas well" shall have the meanings prescribed by applicable law or the appropriate governmental authority, or, if no definition is so prescribed, "oil well" means a well with an initial gas-oil ratio of less than 100,000 cubic feet per barrel and "gas well" means a well with an initial gas-oil ratio of 100,000 cubic feet or more per barrel, based on a 24-hour production test conducted under normal producing conditions using standard lease separator facilities or equivalent testing equipment; and the term "horizontal completion" means a well in which the horizontal component of the completion interval in the reservoir exceeds the vertical component in such interval. In exercising its pooling rights hereunder, Lessee shall file of record a written declaration describing the unit and stating the effective date of pooling. Production, drilling or reworking operations anywhere on a unit which includes all or any part of the leased premises shall be treated as if it were production, drilling or reworking operations on the leased premises, except that the production on which Lessor's royalty is calculated shall be that proportion of the total unit production which the net acreage covered by this lease and included in the unit bears to the total acreage in the unit, but only to the extent such proportion of unit production is sold by Lessee. In the event a unit is formed hereunder before the unit well is drilled and completed, so that the applicable pooling criteria are not yet known, the unit shall be based on the pooling criteria Lessee expects in good faith to apply upon completion of the well; provided that within a reasonable time after completion of the well, the unit shall be revised if necessary to conform to the pooling criteria that actually exist. Pooling in one or more instances shall not exhaust

Lessee's pooling rights hereunder, and Lessee shall have the recurring right but not the obligation to revise any unit formed hereunder by expansion or contraction or both, either before or after commencement of production, in order to conform to the well spacing or density pattern prescribed or permitted by the governmental authority having jurisdiction, or to conform to any productive acreage determination made by such governmental authority. To revise a unit hereunder, Lessee shall file of record a written declaration describing the revised unit and stating the effective date of revision. To the extent any portion of the leased premises is included in or excluded from the unit by virtue of such revision, the proportion of unit production on which royalties are payable hereunder shall thereafter be adjusted accordingly.

Proportionate Reduction Clause

The proportionate reduction clause of an oil and gas lease allows a Lessee to proportionately reduce royalties and rentals to a Lessor, if the Lessor owns less than 100 percent of the mineral rights in the tract of land where a well is located. It may also stipulate that if any royalty or other payment attributable to the mineral estate is payable to someone other than the Lessor, then it will be deducted from the corresponding amount that would otherwise be payable to the Lessor.

Example Proportionate Reduction Clause

If Lessor owns less than the full mineral estate in all or any part of the leased premises, payment of royalties and shut-in royalties hereunder shall be reduced as follows: royalties and shut-in royalties for any well on any part of the leased premises or lands pooled therewith shall be reduced to the proportion that Lessor's interest in such part of the leased premises bears to the full mineral estate in such part of the leased premises. To the extent any royalty or other payment attributable to the mineral estate covered by this lease is payable to someone other than Lessor, such royalty or other payment shall be deducted from the corresponding amount otherwise payable to Lessor hereunder.

Surrender Clause

The surrender clause describes how a Lessee may surrender or release all or part of their interests in a lease to the Lessor.

Example Surrender Clause

Lessee may, at any time and from time

to time, deliver to Lessor or file of record a written release of this lease as to a full or undivided interest in all or any portion of the area covered by this lease or any depths or zones thereunder, and shall thereupon be relieved of all obligations thereafter arising with respect to the interest so released. If Lessee releases less than all of the interest or area covered hereby, Lessee's obligation to pay or tender shut-in royalties shall be proportionately reduced in accordance with the net acreage interest retained hereunder.

Surface Rights Clause

Although the surface interest is servient to the mineral interest, it is always helpful to state specifics in writing. The surface rights clause of an oil and gas lease clearly states the Lessee's rights to use the surface. This includes the rights of ingress and egress on the premises, geophysical operations, drilling wells, building roads, constructing surface production facilities, drilling water wells, disposal wells, and injection wells, adding electrical connections, and the use of water from ponds, lakes, and rivers. Any restrictions on the Lessee's operation are also included such as not operating within 300 feet of a house or a livestock pen. It may also describe a Lessee's right to pull casing and remove surface production facilities even after a lease has terminated in all other respects.

Example Surface Rights Clause

The rights granted to Lessee hereunder shall include the right of ingress and egress on the leased premises or lands pooled or unitized therewith, along with such rights as may be reasonably necessary to conduct operations for exploring, developing, producing and marketing Oil and Gas Substances, including but not limited to geophysical operations, the drilling of wells, and the construction and use of roads, canals, pipelines, tanks, water wells, disposal wells, injection wells, pits, electric and telephone lines, power stations, and other facilities deemed necessary by Lessee to explore, discover, produce, store, treat and/or transport Oil and Gas Substances and water produced from the leased premises or other lands that share central facilities and are jointly operated with the leased premises for gathering, treating, compression and water disposal. Lessee may use in such operations, free of cost, any oil, gas, water and/or other substances produced on the leased premises, except water from Lessor's wells or ponds. In exploring, developing, producing or marketing from the leased premises or lands pooled or unitized therewith, the ancillary rights granted herein shall apply (a) to the entire leased premises, notwithstanding any partial release or other partial termination of this lease; and (b) to any other lands in which Lessor now or hereafter has authority to grant such rights in the vicinity of the leased premises or lands pooled or unitized therewith. When requested by Lessor in writing, Lessee shall bury its pipelines below ordinary plow depth on cultivated lands. No well shall be located less than 200 feet from any house or barn now on the leased premises or other lands of Lessor used by Lessee hereunder, without Lessor's consent, and Lessee shall pay for damage caused by its operations to buildings and other improvements now on the leased premises or such other lands, and to commercial timber and growing crops thereon. Lessee shall have the right at any time to remove its fixtures, equipment and materials, including well casing, from the leased premises or such other lands during the term of this lease or within a reasonable time thereafter.

Unitization Clause

A unitization clause in an oil and gas lease grants the Lessee the right to add the leased premises to a multi-well unit that will include offset leases held by other Operators. This is the first cooperative step that is necessary to initiate a secondary recovery project such as water-flooding where several operators exist in a single field.

Example Unitization Clause

Lessee shall have the right but not the obligation to commit all or any part of the leased premises or interest therein to one or more unit plans or agreements for the cooperative development or operation of one or more oil and/ or gas reservoirs or portions thereof, if in lessee's judgment such plan or agreement will prevent waste and protect correlative rights, and if such plan or agreement is approved by the federal, state or local governmental authority having jurisdiction. When such a commitment is made, this lease shall be subject to the terms and conditions of the unit plan or agreement, including any formula prescribed therein for the allocation of production from a unit. Upon permanent cessation thereof, Lessee may terminate the unit by filing of record a written declaration describing the unit and stating the date of termination. Pooling hereunder shall not constitute a cross-conveyance of interests.

Example Oil and Gas Lease

The following is an example of a paid-up oil and gas lease. The original author of this lease is unknown.

PAID UP OIL AND GAS LEASE

THIS LEASE AGREEMENT is made as of the _____ day of _____, 20__ between _____

_____ as Lessor (whether one or more), and

_____, as Lessee. All printed portions of this lease were prepared by the party hereinabove named as Lessee, but all other provisions (including the completion of blank spaces) were prepared jointly by Lessor and Lessee.

1. Grant of Leased Premises. In consideration of a cash bonus in hand paid and the covenants herein contained

Lessor hereby grants, leases and lets exclusively to Lessee the following described land, hereinafter called leased premises:

(Legal Description Inserted Here)

In the County of

_____/

State of

_____/

Containing_____gross acres,

more or less (including any interests therein which Lessor may hereafter acquire by reversion, prescription or otherwise), for the purpose of exploring for, developing, producing and marketing oil and gas, along with all hydrocarbon and non-hydrocarbon substances produced in association therewith ("Oil and Gas Substances"). The term "gas" as used herein includes helium, carbon dioxide, gaseous sulfur compounds, methane produced from coal formations and other commercial gases, as well as normal hydrocarbon gases. In addition to the above-described land, this lease and the term "leased premises" also covers accretions and any small strips or parcels of land now or hereafter owned by Lessor which are contiguous or adjacent to the above-described land, and, in consideration of the aforementioned cash bonus, Lessor agrees to execute at Lessee's request any additional or supplemental instruments for a more complete or accurate description of the land so covered. For the purpose of determining the amount of any payments based on acreage hereunder, the number of gross acres above specified shall be deemed correct, whether actually more or less.

2. Ancillary Rights. The rights granted to Lessee hereunder shall include the right of ingress and egress on the leased premises or lands pooled or unitized therewith, along with such rights as may be reasonably necessary to conduct operations for exploring, developing, producing and marketing Oil and Gas Substances, including but not limited to geophysical operations, the drilling of wells, and the construction and use of roads, canals, pipelines, tanks, water wells, disposal wells, injection wells, pits, electric and telephone lines, power stations, and other facilities deemed necessary by Lessee to explore, discover, produce, store, treat and/or transport Oil and Gas Substances and water produced from the leased premises or other lands that share central facilities and are jointly

operated with the leased premises
for gathering, treating, compression
and water disposal. Lessee may use in
such operations, free of cost, any oil,
gas, water and/or other substances
produced on the leased premises, except
water from Lessor's wells or ponds. In
exploring, developing, producing or
marketing from the leased premises
or lands pooled or unitized therewith,
the ancillary rights granted herein
shall apply (a) to the entire leased
premises, notwithstanding any partial
release or other partial termination of
this lease; and (b) to any other lands
in which Lessor now or hereafter has
authority to grant such rights in the
vicinity of the leased premises or lands
pooled or unitized therewith. When
requested by Lessor in writing, Lessee
shall bury its pipelines below ordinary
plow depth on cultivated lands. No
well shall be located less than 200 feet
from any house or barn now on the
leased premises or other lands of Lessor

used by Lessee hereunder, without Lessor's consent, and Lessee shall pay for damage caused by its operations to buildings and other improvements now on the leased premises or such other lands, and to commercial timber and growing crops thereon. Lessee shall have the right at any time to remove its fixtures, equipment and materials, including well casing, from the leased premises or such other lands during the term of this lease or within a reasonable time thereafter. Term of Lease. This lease shall be in force for a primary term of _____ years from the date hereof, and for as long thereafter as oil or gas or other substances covered hereby are produced in paying quantities from the leased premises or from lands pooled or unitized therewith or this lease is otherwise maintained in effect pursuant to the provisions hereof.

4. Operations. If Lessee drills a well which is incapable of producing in paying quantities (hereinafter called "dry hole") on the leased premises or lands pooled or unitized therewith, or if all production (whether or not in paying quantities) permanently ceases from any cause, including a revision of unit boundaries pursuant to the provisions of this lease or the action of any governmental authority, then in the event this lease is not otherwise being maintained in force it shall nevertheless remain in force if Lessee commences further operations for reworking an existing well or for drilling an additional well or for otherwise obtaining or restoring production on the leased premises or lands pooled or unitized therewith within 90 days after completion of operations on such dry hole or within 90 days after such cessation of all production. If after the primary term this lease is not otherwise being maintained in force, but Lessee is

then engaged in Operations, as defined below, this lease shall remain in force so long as any one or more of such Operations are prosecuted with no interruption of more than 90 consecutive days, and if any such Operations result in the production of Oil and Gas Substances, as long thereafter as there is production in paying quantities from the leased premises or lands pooled or unitized therewith. After completion of a well capable of producing in paying quantities hereunder, Lessee shall drill such additional wells on the leased premises or lands pooled or unitized therewith as a reasonably prudent operator would drill under the same or similar circumstances to (a) develop the leased premises as to reservoirs then capable of producing in paying quantities on the leased premises or lands pooled or unitized therewith, or (b) protect the leased premises from uncompensated drainage by any well or wells located on other lands not pooled or unitized therewith. There shall be no covenant to drill exploratory wells or any additional wells except as expressly provided herein. As used herein, the term Operations shall mean any activity conducted on or off the leased premises that is reasonably calculated to obtain or restore production, including without limitation, (i) drilling or any act preparatory to drilling (such as obtaining permits, surveying a drill site, staking a drill site, building roads, clearing a drill site, or hauling equipment or supplies); (ii) reworking, plugging back, deepening, treating, stimulating, refitting, installing any artificial lift or production-enhancement equipment or technique; (iii) constructing facilities related to the production, treatment, transportation and marketing of substances produced from the lease premises; (iv) contracting for marketing services and sale of Oil and Gas Substances; and (v) construction of water disposal facilities and the physical movement of water produced from the leased premises.

5. Shut-in Royalty. If after the primary term one or more wells on the leased premises or lands pooled or unitized therewith are capable of producing Oil and Gas Substances in paying quantities, but such well or wells are either shut in or production therefrom is not being sold by Lessee, such well or wells shall nevertheless be deemed to be producing in paying quantities for the purpose of maintaining this lease. If for a period of 90 consecutive days such well or wells are shut in or production therefrom is not sold by Lessee, then Lessee shall pay an aggregate shut-in royalty of one dollar per acre then covered by this lease. The payment shall be made to Lessor on or before the first anniversary date of the lease following the end of the 90day period and thereafter on or before each

anniversary while the well or wells
are shut in or production therefrom
is not being sold by Lessee; provided
that if this lease is otherwise being
maintained by operations under this
lease, or if production is being sold by
Lessee from another well or wells on
the leased premises or lands pooled or
unitized therewith, no shut-in royalty
shall be due until the first anniversary
date of the lease following the end of
the 90day period after the end of the
period next following the cessation of
such operations or production, as the
case may be. Lessee's failure to properly
pay shut-in royalty shall render Lessee
liable for the amount due, but shall not
operate to terminate this lease.

6. Royalty Payment. For all Oil and
Gas Substances that are physically
produced from the leased premises, or
lands pooled, unitized or communitized
therewith, and sold, Lessor shall receive

as its royalty _____ % of the sales proceeds actually received by lessee or, if applicable, its affiliate, as a result of the first sale of the affected production to an unaffiliated party, less this same percentage share of all Post Production Costs and this same percentage share of all production, severance and ad valorem taxes. As used in this provision, Post Production Costs shall mean all costs actually incurred by lessee or its affiliate and all losses of produced volumes whether by use as fuel, line loss, flaring, venting or otherwise from and after the wellhead to the point of sale. These costs include without limitation, all costs of gathering, marketing, compression, dehydration, transportation, removal of liquid or gaseous substances or impurities from the affected production, and any other treatment or processing required by the first unaffiliated party who purchases the affected production. For royalty calculation purposes, lessee shall never be required to adjust the sales proceeds to account for the purchaser's costs or charges downstream of the point of sale.

Lessee or its affiliate shall have the right to construct, maintain and operate any facilities providing some or all of the services identified as Post Production Costs. If this occurs, the actual costs of such facilities shall be included in the Post Production Costs as a per barrel or per mcf charge, as appropriate, calculated by spreading the construction, maintenance and operating costs for such facilities over the reasonably estimated total production volumes attributable to the well or wells using such facilities.

If Lessee uses the Oil and Gas Substances (other than as fuel in connection with the production and sale thereof) in lieu of receiving sale proceeds, the price to be used under this provision shall be based upon arm's-length sale(s) to unaffiliated parties for the applicable month that are obtainable, comparable in terms of quality and quantity, and in closest proximity to the leased premises. Such comparable arm's-length sales price shall be less any Post Production Costs applicable to the specific arms-length transaction that is utilized.

7. Pooling. Lessee shall have the right but not the obligation to pool all or any part of the leased premises or interest therein with any other lands or interests, as to any or all depths or zones, and as to any or all substances covered by this lease, either before or after the commencement of drilling or production, whenever Lessee deems it necessary or proper to do so in order to prudently develop or operate the leased premises, whether or not similar pooling authority exists with respect to such other lands or interests. The creation of a unit by such pooling shall be based

on the following criteria (hereinafter
called "pooling criteria"): A unit for
an oil well (other than a horizontal
completion) shall not exceed 40 acres
plus a maximum acreage tolerance of
10%, and for a gas well or a horizontal
completion shall not exceed 640 acres
plus a maximum acreage tolerance of
10%; provided that a larger unit may
be formed for an oil well or gas well
or horizontal completion to conform
to any well spacing or density pattern
that may be prescribed or permitted
by any governmental authority having
jurisdiction to do so. For the purpose
of the foregoing, the terms "oil well"
and "gas well" shall have the meanings
prescribed by applicable law or the
appropriate governmental authority,
or, if no definition is so prescribed, "oil
well" means a well with an initial gas-
oil ratio of less than 100,000 cubic feet
per barrel and "gas well" means a well
with an initial gas-oil ratio of 100,000
cubic feet or more per barrel, based on

a 24-hour production test conducted under normal producing conditions using standard lease separator facilities or equivalent testing equipment; and the term "horizontal completion" means a well in which the horizontal component of the completion interval in the reservoir exceeds the vertical component in such interval. In exercising its pooling rights hereunder, Lessee shall file of record a written declaration describing the unit and stating the effective date of pooling. Production, drilling or reworking operations anywhere on a unit which includes all or any part of the leased premises shall be treated as if it were production, drilling or reworking operations on the leased premises, except that the production on which Lessor's royalty is calculated shall be that proportion of the total unit production which the net acreage covered by this lease and included in the unit bears to the total acreage in the unit, but only to the extent such proportion of unit production is sold by Lessee. In the event a unit is formed hereunder before the unit well is drilled and completed, so that the applicable pooling criteria are not yet known, the unit shall be based on the pooling criteria Lessee expects in good faith to apply upon completion of the well; provided that within a reasonable time after completion of the well, the unit shall be revised if necessary to conform to the pooling criteria that actually exist. Pooling in one or more instances shall not exhaust Lessee's pooling rights hereunder, and Lessee shall have the recurring right but not the obligation to revise any unit formed hereunder by expansion or contraction or both, either before or after commencement of production, in order to conform to the well spacing or density pattern prescribed or permitted by the governmental authority having jurisdiction, or to conform to any productive acreage determination made by such governmental authority. To revise a unit hereunder, Lessee shall file of record a written declaration describing the revised unit and stating the effective date of revision. To the extent any portion of the leased premises is included in or excluded from the unit by virtue of such revision, the proportion of unit production on which royalties are payable hereunder shall thereafter be adjusted accordingly.

8. Unitization. Lessee shall have the right but not the obligation to commit all or any part of the leased premises or interest therein to one or more unit plans or agreements for the cooperative development or operation of one or more oil and/or gas reservoirs or portions thereof, if in lessee's judgment such plan or agreement will prevent waste and protect correlative rights, and if such plan or agreement is approved by the federal, state or

local governmental authority having jurisdiction. When such a commitment is made, this lease shall be subject to the terms and conditions of the unit plan or agreement, including any formula prescribed therein for the allocation of production from a unit. Upon permanent cessation thereof, Lessee may terminate the unit by filing of record a written declaration describing the unit and stating the date of termination. Pooling hereunder shall not constitute a cross-conveyance of interests.

9. Payment Reductions. If Lessor owns less than the full mineral estate in all or any part of the leased premises, payment of royalties and shut-in royalties hereunder shall be reduced as follows: royalties and shut-in royalties for any well on any part of the leased premises or lands pooled therewith shall be reduced to the proportion

that Lessor's interest in such part of the leased premises bears to the full mineral estate in such part of the leased premises. To the extent any royalty or other payment attributable to the mineral estate covered by this lease is payable to someone other than Lessor, such royalty or other payment shall be deducted from the corresponding amount otherwise payable to Lessor hereunder.

10. Ownership Changes. The interest of either Lessor or Lessee hereunder may be assigned, devised or otherwise transferred in whole or in part, by area and/or by depth or zone, and the rights and obligations of the parties hereunder shall extend to their respective heirs, devisees, executors, administrators, successors and assigns. No change in Lessor's ownership shall have the effect of reducing the rights or enlarging the obligations of Lessee hereunder, and no

change in ownership shall be binding on Lessee until 60 days after Lessee has been furnished the original or duly authenticated copies of the documents establishing such change of ownership to the satisfaction of Lessee or until Lessor has satisfied the notification requirements contained in Lessee's usual form of division order. In the event of the death of any person entitled to shut-in royalties hereunder, Lessee may pay or tender such shut-in royalties to the credit of decedent or decedent's estate. If at any time two or more persons are entitled to shut-in royalties hereunder, Lessee may pay or tender such shut-in royalties to such persons either jointly or separately in proportion to the interest which each owns. If Lessee transfers its interest hereunder in whole or in part Lessee shall be relieved of all obligations thereafter arising with respect to the transferred interest, and failure of the transferee to satisfy such obligations with respect to the transferred interest shall not affect the rights of Lessee with respect to any interest not so transferred. If Lessee transfers a full or undivided interest in all or any portion of the area covered by this lease, the obligation to pay or tender shut-in royalties hereunder shall be divided between Lessee and the transferee in proportion to the net acreage interest in this lease then held by each.

11. Release of Lease. Lessee may, at any time and from time to time, deliver to Lessor or file of record a written release of this lease as to a full or undivided interest in all or any portion of the area covered by this lease or any depths or zones thereunder, and shall thereupon be relieved of all obligations thereafter arising with respect to the interest so released. If Lessee releases less than all of the interest or area covered hereby, Lessee's obligation to

pay or tender shut-in royalties shall be proportionately reduced in accordance with the net acreage interest retained hereunder.

12. Regulation and Delay. Lessee's obligations under this lease, whether express or implied, shall be subject to all applicable laws, rules, regulations and orders of any governmental authority having jurisdiction, including restrictions on the drilling and production of wells, and regulation of the price or transportation of oil, gas and other substances covered hereby. When drilling, reworking, production or other operations are prevented or delayed by such laws, rules, regulations or orders, or by inability to obtain necessary permits, equipment, services, material, water, electricity, fuel, access or easements, or by fire, flood, adverse weather conditions, war, sabotage, rebellion, insurrection, riot, strike or

labor disputes, or by inability to obtain a satisfactory market for production or failure of purchasers or carriers to take or transport such production, or by any other cause not reasonably within Lessee's control, this lease shall not terminate because of such prevention or delay, and, at Lessee's option, the period of such prevention or delay shall be added to the term hereof. Lessee shall not be liable for breach of any provisions or implied covenants of this lease when drilling, production or other operations are so prevented or delayed.

13. Breach or Default. No litigation shall be initiated by Lessor for damages, forfeiture or cancellation with respect to any breach or default by Lessee hereunder, for a period of at least 90 days after Lessor has given Lessee written notice fully describing the breach or default, and then only if Lessee fails to remedy the breach or

default within such period. In the event the matter is litigated and there is a final judicial determination that a breach or default has occurred, this lease shall not be forfeited or cancelled in whole or in part unless Lessee is given a reasonable time after said judicial determination to remedy the breach or default and Lessee fails to do so.

14. Warranty of Title. Lessor hereby warrants and agrees to defend title conveyed to Lessee hereunder, and agrees that Lessee at Lessee's option may pay and discharge any taxes, mortgages or liens existing, levied or assessed on or against the leased premises. If Lessee exercises such option, Lessee shall be subrogated to the rights of the party to whom payment is made, and, in addition to its other rights, may reimburse itself out of any royalties or shut-in royalties otherwise payable to Lessor hereunder. In the

event Lessee is made aware of any claim inconsistent with Lessor's title, Lessee may suspend the payment of royalties and shut-in royalties hereunder, without interest, until Lessee has been furnished satisfactory evidence that such claim has been resolved.

15. Indemnity. Lessee will indemnify and hold Lessor, its officers, directors, employees, agents, successors and assigns (hereafter collectively referred to as "Indemnified Parties") harmless from any and all claims, demands, suits, losses, damages, and costs (including, without limitation, any attorney fees) incurred by the Indemnified Parties which may be asserted against the Indemnified Parties by reason of or which may arise out of or which may be related to Lessee's activities on the leased premises (including, without limitation, any claims by any owners or lessees of minerals that Lessee's

operations hereunder are either illegal, unauthorized, or constitute an improper interference with their rights).

16. Other Provisions. Additional terms of this Lease are set forth on Exhibit A attached hereto and incorporated herein by reference.

Chapter 4

Questions to Ask Before You Sign an Oil and Gas Lease

Here are a few questions to ask the Land Man who is approaching you about leasing your land. These are also good questions to ask yourself when you are reading a lease. Be sure of the answers.

What land tract or tracts are included in this lease? The legal description of the land should be provided in the lease. There may also be a "Mother Hubbard" clause which will include any small pieces of land that are adjacent to the main tract that is described in the legal description so that all of the mineral rights that are owned by the Lessor in that particular location are included in the lease regardless of whether or not they are perfectly described in the legal description that is in the lease.

What is the gross acreage that will be assumed to be covered by this lease? Certain payments such as delay rentals and shut-in royalties may be dependent on the number of acres that are leased and often a lease will state the number of acres that are assumed to be covered for these purposes so that the parties do not have to know the exact acreage down to the fraction of a square foot. Such a clause if called an In Gross Provision.

What substances are covered by the lease? Most Oil and Gas Leases include oil, gas, and other hydrocarbons.
But does this lease also include other minerals that are not hydrocarbons? The term gas may be defined to include gaseous substances that are not hydrocarbons. For example, helium is a valuable gaseous substance that is not a hydrocarbon.

How long is the Primary Term of the lease? A typical length of the primary term is three years. Some leases are longer and some are shorter.

How can the lease be extended beyond the primary term? Almost all leases can be extended beyond the primary term by drilling at least one well that produces oil and or natural gas in paying quantities.

Are delay rentals due during the primary term to keep the lease in effect if wells are not drilled and producing in paying quantities? Delay rentals will be due unless it is a Paid Up Lease.

What happens if the oil company drills a dry hole? The dry hole and cessation of production clause in and Oil and Gas Lease describes how a lease can be maintained if a dry hole is drilled. If there are no other producing wells the oil company usually has an opportunity to drill another well within a specified period of time – usually 90 to 180 days. If the primary term has ended and they do not begin drilling the next well within the specified period of time, the lease usually terminates.

Is this a Paid-Up Lease or is there a rental clause? If a lease is a Paid-Up lease it means that once the lease is signed and the initial lease bonus is paid then no more payments are necessary to keep the lease in effect until the end of the primary term which may be several years. If a lease is not a Paid-Up Lease then there will usually be a rental clause that describes how delay rentals (Annual Payments) can be paid that will keep the lease in effect during the primary term. If the delay rentals are not paid and no well is producing in paying quantities then the lease expires.

What is the Royalty? This is the most important question. The Royalty Clause describes exactly how the Mineral Interest Royalty will be calculated. Royalties are usually a fixed percentage of the net proceeds of product sales. Adjustments are often made for the Lessor's (your) proportionate share of state and county taxes on oil and gas production sales. In other words, you may be asked to pay your share of the taxes on production. Generally royalties are free of the cost of bringing the product to the surface but can be adjusted for the proportionate cost, if any, of getting the product from the wellhead to the point of sale. These are called post-production costs.

Is there a Shut-In Royalty Clause? A shut-in royalty clause of an Oil and Gas Lease describes how payments may be made to a Lessor by a Lessee if a well is shut-in. Payment of shut-in royalties allows the Lessee to maintain the lease in full force as if the well were producing in paying quantities. A limiting clause may be included that limits the amount of time that a lease may be maintained by shut-in royalties.

Is there a Pooling Clause? A pooling clause in an Oil and Gas Lease enables a Lessee to combine several leases in to a single one-well unit as may be required to meet the spacing requirements of the state oil and gas regulatory agency.

Is there a Surface Rights Clause?

Although the surface interest is servient to the mineral interest, it is always helpful state specifics in writing. The surface rights clause of an Oil and Gas Lease clearly states the Lessee's rights to use the surface. This includes the rights of ingress and egress on the premises, geophysical operations, drilling wells, building roads, constructing surface production facilities, drilling water wells, disposal wells, and injection wells, adding electrical connections, and the use of water from ponds, lakes, and rivers. Any restrictions on the Lessee's operation are also included such as not operating within 300 feet of a house or a livestock pen. It may also describe a Lessee's right to pull casing and remove surface production facilities even after a lease has terminated in all other respects.

Is there a Unitization Clause? A unitization clause in an Oil and Gas Lease grants the Lessee the right to add the leased premises to a multi-well unit that will include offset leases held by other Operators. This is the first cooperative step that is necessary to initiate a secondary recovery project such as water-flooding where several operators exist in a single field.

Is there a Pugh Clause? A Pugh clause in an Oil and Gas Lease limits the acreage in a lease that may be held by production after the primary term. Any leased lands where wells have not been drilled and operations are not taking place will be released from the lease. Here is an example of a Pugh Clause. "If at the end of the primary term, a part but not all of the land covered by this lease, on a surface acreage basis, is not included within a unit or units in accordance with the other provisions hereof, this lease shall terminate as to such part, or parts, of the land lying outside such unit or units, unless this lease is perpetuated as to such land outside such unit or units by operations conducted thereon or by the production of oil, gas or other minerals, or by such operations and such production in accordance with the provisions hereof." While many leases have Pugh clauses they are looked upon unfavorably by oil companies and their potential partners. Having a Pugh clause in your lease makes your project less attractive to capital investors. Try to talk this over with your potential Lessee. Find out what they really need in terms of time and acreage for full-scale development of your acreage. If you want them to invest the time and money that is required to shoot seismic over your property then you have to give them the time they need to drill all of the wells. If you cut their acreage position after just three years down to the minimum amount required by the state they and all of their potential partners will look at your project less favorably. Perhaps each well they drill during the first three years will earn them an additional three years of primary term on an abstract or survey of their choice. There has to be a clear path for them to succeed on a large scale over time or they will not make the large investments that are required at the beginning. This is a clause where you can be stubborn and inadvertently harm your own interests. But you do not want an oil company to potentially hold portions of your property for decades if they are not producing from it and have no intention of developing it.

Glossary

Abstract Number - The land in every County in Texas is broken up in to parcels called abstracts and every abstract has an abstract number. Parcels of land within a county in Texas may be identified by their abstract number. A parcel of land with an abstract number of 500 is often expressed in writing as A-500. The land within a particular abstract may be entirely own by one party or it may be subdivided in to smaller tracts of land that are each owned by one or more parties.

Abstract of Title - The history of ownership of a tract of land. It may include all of the title conveyance documents associated with the property going all the way back to sovereignty (the time when the land was owned by the state).

Acidizing - An operation in which a strong acid such as Hydrochloric Acid (HCl) is pumped down a wellbore, through perforations in the casing, and in to a formation. The purpose of the operation is to dissolve calcite near the wellbore and in fractures that connect to the wellbore so that oil gas can flow in to the well bore at higher rates. Acidizing is usually performed in limestone formations or in other formations that contain a significant amount of calcite. Acidizing operations may be performed immediately after perforating a newly drilled well or at any time during the productive life of a well.

Acre - A unit of measurement of land area. The amount of land area in an oil and gas lease is usually measured in acres. An acre is 43,560 square feet. A square mile contains 640 acres. The most common drilling and spacing unit required by the Texas Railroad Commission to drill a shallow oil well is 40 acres. A 40-acre square is 1,320 feet along each side.

Ad Coelum - The common law doctrine that a property owner owns everything on their property from the blue sky all the way to the core of the Earth. This doctrine is still observed with respect to solid minerals but it has been replaced by the "Rule of Capture" for fugacious minerals including oil and gas.

AFE - Also known as an Authorization For Expenditure, an AFE is a document, usually prepared by an Operator to be presented to non-operating working interest owners in a petroleum property that describes a proposed operation, estimated costs of the operation, and an economic justification for the operation. By submitting an AFE to the non-operating working interest owners, an Operator intends to gain their approval to conduct the proposed operation and their agreement to pay their proportionate costs of the operation.

Annulus - The annulus is the space between two concentric cylinders within a wellbore. While a well is being drilled, the annulus is the space between the outside edge of the drill pipe and the borehole wall. In a completed well, the tubing-casing annulus is the space between the outside edge of the tubing and the interior wall of the casing. An annulus also exists between the outside surface of production casing and the inside surface of larger diameter intermediate casing. The annulus is sometime referred to as the "back side".

Anticline - An anticline is a subsurface structure resembling an upside down bowl. An anticline is one of the simplest structures for trapping hydrocarbons. As hydrocarbons migrate up dip, they accumulate in the top of the anticline. Thus the tops of anticlines are ideal places to drill oil and gas wells.

API - The American Petroleum Institute in an oil and gas industry organization that sets standards for oil and gas equipment, recommends certain operating practices, contributes to safety, and publishes documents to aid policy makers. Visit www.api.org

API Gravity - A measure of the density of oil in degrees.

API Gravity = (141.5/Specific Gravity of the Oil at 60 degrees F) - 131.5

Crude oils with an API gravity of 35-50 degrees are light crude oils. Crude oils with an API gravity of 20-35 degrees are medium crude oils. And crude oils with an API gravity of 10-20 degrees are considered heavy crudes.

API Number - Since the 1970's, most wells drilled in the United States have been assigned a unique identification number at the time they were drilled called an API number. The first two digits of the number are determined by the state where the well is located. The next three digits are determined by the county that the well is located in. And the final five digits are unique to each individual well.

Artificial Lift - When the reservoir pressure is not sufficient to push oil and gas from the reservoir all the way to the surface, fluids will not flow to the surface naturally. They may rise to some level within the well but they will not reach the surface. In cases such as this the Operator will use one of several methods of lifting the liquids to the surface. These methods include rod pumps with pump jacks at the surface, gas lift, and electric submersible pumps.

Authorization For Expenditure - Also known as an AFE. This is a document, usually prepared by an Operator to be presented to non-operating working interest owners in a petroleum property that describes a proposed operation, estimated costs of the operation, and an economic justification for the operation. By submitting an AFE to the non-operating working interest owners, an Operator intends to gain their approval to conduct the proposed operation and their agreement to pay their proportionate costs of the operation.

Back In - The right to receive an interest in a petroleum property in the future if certain contractually specified conditions are met. The interest that a party may obtain from a Back In is known as a reversionary interest.

Back In After Pay Out - A particular kind of Back In where a party such as an Independent Geologist, Deal Finder, or Investment Promoter receives a working interest in a petroleum property (a well or group of wells) after it has produced enough money to pay back the initial costs of drilling and completing the well or wells to the working interest owners who paid those expenses. Back in after payout is sometimes abbreviated as (BIAPO).

Barrel - A barrel is a unit of volume equal to 42 gallons. Oil quantities are most often measured in barrels. A barrel is abbreviated as "bbl" or "BBL" or sometime "BO" which means barrels of oil. A barrel is equal to 5.6145833 cubic feet.

Basement - The "Basement" is igneous rock of Pre-Cambrian age that underlies Phanerozoic sedimentary rock throughout most of the world. It is usually granite. Most sedimentary rocks in the world are of Paleozoic, Mesozoic, or Cenozoic age - which means they are 0 to 542 million years old. Rocks created more the 542 million years ago were formed during a period of Earth's history known as the Pre-Cambrian time. They tend to be non-sedimentary rocks such as granite and they rarely contain oil and gas. Thus, drilling operations usually cease when a well bore penetrates all of the younger rocks that were deposited between zero and 542 million years ago and then enters the "Basement" which is more than 542 million years old. Experience and conventional thinking says that there is very little to be gained from drilling in the "Basement".

Basin - A basin is a natural depression in the Earth's surface resulting from tectonic activity. A basin is many miles or kilometers in width. Over many millions of years sediments from rocks in higher positions around the basin are eroded and grains are transported by water, wind, or glaciers in to the basin. After these layers of sediments accumulate and are gradually buried by subsequent sediments, they are later lithified to form sedimentary rock. Hydrocarbons may later migrate up through the rock and become trapped in certain local structures or simply within certain permeable strata. It is for this reason that basins full of sedimentary rock are target areas for oil and gas exploration. Hundreds of basins have been identified throughout the world. The largest oil and gas producing basin in the lower 48 states is the Permian Basin which is filled with sediments of Paleozoic age.

BCF - Billion Cubic Feet. A BCF is a unit of measurement of natural gas volume meaning one billion cubic feet of gas at standard conditions of 1 atmosphere of pressure and 60 degrees Fahrenheit. If natural gas is selling for $5.00 per thousand cubic feet (MCF), then one million cubic feet (MMCF) is worth $5,000.00 and one billion cubic feet (BCF) is worth $5 million.

Behind Pipe - A terms that refers to oil and gas reserves in a particular formation that is accessible within an existing wellbore where casing has been set, but where no attempt has yet been made to perforate the casing at the depth of that formation to produce those reserves of oil and gas. Such reserves of oil and gas are said to be "behind pipe". If a well is drilled and multiple pay zones are encountered and production casing is run. The Operator will usually begin by producing the deepest pay zone first and then moving up the well and producing each additional pay zone one-by-one. In such a case while the deepest zone is being produced first. All of the other zones would be described as reserves "Behind Pipe".

Blue Sky Laws - State laws relating to the sale of securities such as interests in an oil well. Blue Sky Laws are designed to protect the assets of financially uneducated and inexperienced persons.

Bonus - A sum of money paid by the Lessee (Oil Company) to a Lessor (Mineral Interest Owner) as an incentive and as good and valuable consideration at the time an oil and gas lease is executed (signed) by a Lessor. The amount is negotiable and is often based on a certain number of dollars per acre of land being leased.

Borehole - The hole or pathway created by drilling a well in to the ground.

BS & W - Base settlement and water. When crude oil is brought to the surface and stored in an oil stock tank, a small amount of water and solids will usually accumulate on the bottom of the tank because the oil is not completely pure.

The BS&W has no economic value and its volume, if any, is excluded when calculating the amount payable when oil is sold from one party to another.

Calcite - The mineral calcium carbonate Ca CO_3. Calcite is the primary component of limestone. It can also exist as cement in a sandstone formation. Calcite fizzes with bubbles when drops of hydrochloric acid (HCL) are placed on it. This is a means of distinguishing calcite from dolomite which does not fizz.

Caliper Log - A log that measures the diameter of the inside of a wellbore at various depths. It is usually a continuous series of measurements that are three to six inches apart within a well over a planned interval that can be thousands of feet in length. Caliper logging tools may have a single arm that produces a simple one-dimensional measurement or they may have many arms extending from the tool that measure in multiple azimuths and create a three-dimensional image of the borehole wall. Caliper logs can be run in open hole or cased hole. Drillers often use caliper logs to calculate the amount of cement they must pump behind the casing when they run a string of casing in open hole. Production Engineers sometimes use caliper logs in cased holes to identify wear on the inside of the casing. Caliper logs can be acquired with both mechanical fingers and acoustic travel time measurements.

Carried Interest - Also called a "carry". A carried interest is an interest that is converted to a working interest if and when certain previously negotiated conditions are met. When the conversion occurs, the existing working interest owners jointly and proportionately surrender a portion of their working interest to create room for the new working interest that is owned by the new party. The owner of a carried interest does not receive revenue from that interest and is not liable for costs associated with the interest until the time that the carried interest is converted to a working interest.

The three most common conditions or times when a carried interest is converted to a working interest are (1) when a well has been drilled to the casing point, (2) when a well has been drilled and casing and surface facilities have been set and the well is about to begin production ("A Carried Interest Through the Tanks"), and (3) at the time the costs of drilling and completing a well have been recouped by the initial working interest owners or investors. This point in time is also known as "Pay Out" or "Project Pay Out". This third arrangement is known as a Back In After Pay Out (BIAPO). After the conversion of a carried interest to a working interest occurs, all parties pay their proportionate share of all expenses going forward. The parties are said to be proceeding "Heads Up" which means no one is being carried and everyone is paying their proportionate share of expenses and receiving their proportionate share of the Net Revenue

Interest (NRI).

Cased Hole - A well where casing has been run. The opposite of a cased hole is an open hole. An open hole is a borehole where casing has not been run.

Casing - Pipe, usually made of steel, that is inserted along the entire length of a borehole to preserve the borehole and prevent collapse or cave-in of the surrounding rock. It also prevents unwanted fluids from entering the well from depths above or below the pay zones. Casing must be designed to withstand internal bursting pressure, external collapse pressure and the tension resulting from the buoyed weight of all of the casing hanging below each joint. The American Petroleum Institute (www.api.org) has developed design standards for casing. These provide standard diameters and standardized strengths.

Casing and tubing are described by their outside diameter (OD), weight per foot, and API metal grade such as J-55, L-80, N-80, or P-110. The thicker the casing wall, the smaller the inside diameter (ID) and the higher the weight per foot. Common casing diameters range from 2-7/8 inches to 13-3/8 inches. Casing strings are designed from the bottom up with safety factors for burst, collapse, and tension. Casing should be set in tension at the surface in order to prevent buckling down hole. Most casing comes from the mill in joints that are approximately 40 feet in length.

Casing Point - The point in time when a well has been drilled to its planned total depth and the working interest owners must decide whether to run production casing and complete the well or to plug and abandon the well as a dry hole.

Christmas Tree – An assembly of valves and fittings at the top of a well that is used to control the flow of fluids produced from the well. It is visible at the top of a well and is most commonly spoken about regarding gas wells.

Circulating - Pumping drilling fluid down the inside of drill pipe, casing, or tubing and back up to the surface through the annulus. When an Operator is drilling a well using a rotary rig, the Operator is almost always circulating while drilling. The flow of drilling fluid down the inside of the drill pipe, through jets in the drill bit and then back up the annulus serves several purposes. First, it cools the drill bit. Second, it clears the chunks of rock that the bit cuts (called cuttings) from the surface where the drill bit is cutting so that the drill bit can efficiently continue to drill ahead. And third, the circulating drilling fluid lifts the cuttings to the surface so that the borehole is clear. The cuttings are removed from the drilling fluid on the surface by passing the fluid across a shale shaker.

Note: It is at or near the shale shaker where Mud Loggers obtain their cutting samples.

Circulating may also be performed in a cased hole wherein completion fluid is pumped down the inside of tubing and then back up the tubing-casing annulus.

Circulating System - A circulating system is an integral part of every rotary drilling rig. It consists of a mud pit or mud tanks, pumps, a stand pipe in the derrick, a mud hose connecting the stand pipe to the top of the kelly, the drill string, shale shakers, and sometimes a mud gas separator.

Circulating Bottoms Up - Circulating for a sufficient period of time to allow the drilling fluid that is at the bottom of the wellbore at the time the Operator begins circulating to be returned to the surface. An Operator will often "Circulate Bottoms Up" when they have drilled a well to its planned depth but before beginning to trip out of the hole with the drill pipe and drill bit. This is one last effort to clean the wellbore and remove any cuttings or mud balls before tripping out of the hole to run wireline logs and then casing.

Completion - All of the operations that are conducted in a well after a well has been drilled and evaluated and a decision has been made to attempt to produce oil and gas from the well. Completion operations prepare a well to begin producing. Completions includes such operations as perforating, stimulating the well by hydraulic fracturing, acidizing, running downhole equipment such as tubing, plugs, packers, sucker rods, pumps, and other artificial lift equipment.

Condensate - Also known as distillate. Condensates are hydrocarbons that exist in a gaseous phase while in the reservoir at natural reservoir temperature and pressure but later condense in to a liquid phase when they are brought to the surface where pressures and temperatures are lower. Changes in temperature and pressure can occur as these hydrocarbons are traveling up the wellbore toward the surface and when they are on the surface. Condensed liquids are usually low in density and relatively clear or transparent in appearance. A condensate gas reservoir is a gas reservoir that contains some hydrocarbons that will condense in to liquid phase when brought to the surface and allowed to assume lower pressures and temperatures. Condensate is very valuable. An Operator will take steps to insure that condensate is captured at the surface and sold.

Core Sample - A core sample is a sample of rock from a subsurface formation. Core samples or "cores" may be obtained in three ways. The first method involves using a cylindrical shaped drill bit called a core bit that has a rough cutting surface around its bottom edge and cylindrical hole in its center. It is attached to the bottom of the drill string in lieu of a standard bit. As the core bit rotates it cuts a cylindrically shaped hole in the rock and leaves a smaller segment of rock in the center untouched. The core bit swallows the rock in the center and that rock is later brought to surface. A similar feat could be achieved by thrusting the open end of a drinking straw in to mashed potatoes and then withdrawing the straw. You would obtain a "core sample" of mashed potatoes inside the straw. Core samples from a well are usually 3-6 inches in diameter and can be tens to hundreds of feet in length. A core sample obtained in this way is called a whole core. Coring in this way is perhaps the best means of formation evaluation because you can see the rock, it grains, its pores, its composition, its post depositional history, and the pore fluids.

If you are searching for oil you can place the core samples under a fluorescent light and those cores that contain oil will fluoresce and appear bright yellow like a yellow highlighter pen. They may also smell like oil! The Bureau of Economic Geology in Texas has huge facilities in Houston, Austin, and Midland that store over 2 million boxes of core samples that have been recovered from thousands of wells in Texas. The facilities are open to the public so you can visit these facilities and view any of these core samples.

Smaller core samples can also be obtained using wireline tools. There are two types. Rotary sidewall coring tools which use a tiny core bit and an electric motor that drills and recovers cores from the side of a wellbore.

And finally percussion sidewall coring tools use a propellant to force small metal cups into the side of a wellbore. The cups are then pulled out of the rock using a pair of cables. Percussion sidewall coring is the least expensive of the three methods. The jarring action makes the cores unsuitable for permeability measurements but they are very useful for quickly determining whether or not a particular zone contains oil and gas or not.

Crude Oil - Also known as crude. Crude oil is a natural mixture of liquid hydrocarbons as it exists underground and when it is brought to the surface. Crude oil is oil that has not been processed in a refinery. Crude oil varies widely in its composition and its physical properties of color, density, and viscosity. Crude oils contain alkanes, naphthenes, and aromatic hydrocarbons. If a crude oil is designated as sweet it means that it does not contain H_2S. If a crude oil is described as sour it means that it contains appreciable amounts of H_2S. Sweet crude is preferable because it costs less to refine. Futures contracts for crude oil are traded in the CME Group.

Cuttings - Small pieces of rock produced by the cutting action of a drill bit as it drills through a formation. Cuttings are cleared from the rock face beneath the drill bit and lifted to the surface by the circulation of drilling fluid down the inside to the drill pipe and back up the annulus. The annulus is the space between the borehole wall and the outside of the drill pipe. Cuttings are removed from the drilling fluid at the surface using a device called a shale shaker. A Mud Logger analyzes cuttings recovered at the surface for lithology and the presence of oil, water, and gas.

Day Work Drilling Contract - A contractual arrangement between an Operator and a Drilling Contractor where the Operator hires and directs the Drilling Contractor in the Drilling of a well and the Operator pays the Drilling Contractor an agreed amount per day as compensation.

Delay Rental - A payment made by the Lessee (Oil Company) to the Lessor (Mineral Rights Owner) of an oil and gas lease that extends the primary term of the lease and thus extends the time that the Lessee has available to begin drilling on the lease premises. A "Paid Up Lease" is an oil and gas lease that does not include provisions for Delay Rentals. In a "Paid Up Lease" the primary term is set at the time the lease is executed and no delay rental payments are ever required.

Depletion - The normal process of removing oil and gas from a reservoir. When a reservoir is depleted there is less oil and gas remaining in the ground and the reservoir pressures are often less than they were before the well or wells were drilled. However, in the case of water drive oil or gas reservoirs the reservoir pressure may remain relatively constant as the oil and gas are depleted because the water moves in to fill the void left by the hydrocarbons that are produced.

Depletion Allowance - The lawfully prescribed deduction of a certain percentage of an Operator's production when calculating U.S. federal income taxes due from oil and gas production operations. This tax benefit of oil and gas investing flows through to working interest owners including investors in oil and gas wells. The depletion allowance for small oil companies is currently 15%. The democrat party in the United States eternally seeks to remove this deduction while the Republican Party eternally defends it.

Dip - The angle of a layer of sedimentary rock relative to horizontal. Horizontal layers of rock are said to have a dip of zero degrees. If beds were thrusted to a point that they were completely vertical they would have a dip of 90 degrees. Most underground formations are somewhere in between. While most sedimentary rock is deposited in horizontal layers those layers can be tilted later as a result of tectonic activity. Dip is important to Oil and Gas Operators because oil floats on water and gas floats on oil. If oil, gas, and water are present in permeable layers of rock, and the rock is tilted or is dipping in one direction, the oil and gas will naturally migrate "up dip" to the higher end of the rock because oil and gas float on water. Operators are often trying to determine which direction is up dip of existing productions so they can drill more wells. Moving down dip would increase the odds of drilling in a portion of the rock that is completely saturated with water rather than oil and gas. You can observe this same phenomenon by filling a bottle half-and-half with oil and water and then holding the bottle horizontally but slightly tilted. The oil will accumulate in the higher end of the bottle and the water will accumulate in the lower end of the bottle.

Dip Log - A dip log is a wireline log or LWD log that measures the dip of the formations that surround a wellbore. Dip log tools often have six arms that extend radially from the tool with pads on them that detect the formations as they pass by. There are also three-dimensional resistivity logging tools that can measure formation dip without touching the borehole wall. These can be useful in rugose (rough) or washed out boreholes. Knowing the dip of a pay zone can suggest which direction to go to drill the next well. Dip logs can also be used to gain clues about the structures of the formations that a well penetrates.

Directional Drilling - Directional drilling means intentionally drilling a wellbore that is not vertical. This includes deviated wells and horizontal wells. An Operator may drill a deviated (non-vertical) well for several reasons.

First, the Operator is unable to position a drilling rig directly above the target because of an obstruction on surface such as a lake, river, airport, or building. Second, an Operator may want to drill a well through two or more subsurface targets that do not lie directly above and below each another. A directional well would be required to drill through those targets. And finally an Operator may wish to drill horizontally. This may be done to maximize production rates by maximizing the surface area of the pay zone that is exposed to the wellbore or to maximize the number of natural fractures in a pay zone that are penetrated by a wellbore. The trajectory of a directional well can be monitored and controlled while it is being drilled through the use of MWD tools (Measurement While Drilling tools).

Division Order - A division order is a document that lists all of the people and entities that have an interest in a well and their numerical interest. The list includes mineral interest owners, overriding royalty interest owners, and working interest owners. A division order directs the payment of proceeds from the sale of produced products to the appropriate parties in the correct percentages.

Downhole Anything that exists or occurs within a wellbore below the surface of the Earth is downhole.

Drill Bit - The device attached to the bottom of the drill string that is used to crush and scrape rock to create a borehole. Rotary Drill bits are available in two broad groups: rolling cutter and drag bits. The most common roller cutter bits are tri-cone rolling cutter bits. Tri-cone rolling cutter bits have three rolling cones with teeth mounted on them that roll on the rock face at the bottom of the wellbore to crush, grind, and scrape the rock. Drag Bits have no moving parts. They have fixed blades finished with extremely strong metal alloys such as tungsten carbide that scrape the rock as the bit turns. Sometimes the blades have industrial diamonds inserted along their edges that assist in tearing the rock as the bit turns. The number of blades on a drag bit ranges from two to seven. The choice of a drill bit depends on the kind of rock that is expected and the amount of footage that the Operator intends to drill through. A drill bit may be purchased from a bit manufacturer or rented. If rented, the price is usually for an agreed amount per foot that the drill bit is used to drill.

Drill Pipe - Metal pipe that is used to drill a well. Drill pipe is specially made for the purpose of turning the drill bit. It connects the drilling rig at the surface to the drill bit that is turning at the bottom of the well. Each section of drill pipe is called a joint of drill pipe or simply a joint. Each joint is approximately 30 feet long. Joints of drill pipe are threaded with a male connection on one end and a female connection on the other end so that they can be connected in a string of pipe thousands of feet in length. A long string of drill pipe connected end to end in a well is called a drill string.

Drill pipe is hollow so that drilling fluid can be pumped down the inside of the pipe, through the bit, and back up the annulus to the surface. The male end is called the pin and the female end is called the box. Drill pipe usually has a greater wall thickness than tubing and casing because it is subjected to abusive torque, vibration, compression, and tension during drilling operations.

This is especially true when drill pipe is beginning to stick or is stuck. Drill pipe ranges in diameter from 3-1/2 inches to 6-1/2 inches. A drilling rig that is tall enough to pull two 30-foot joints of drill pipe (60 feet) at a time and stand them back in the derrick is called a "Double". A drilling rig that is tall enough to pull three 30-foot joints of drill pipe (90 ft) at a time and stand them back in the derrick is called a "Triple".

Drill String - Joints of drill pipe are threaded with a male connection on one end and a female connection on the other end so that they can be connected in a string of pipe thousands of feet in length. The string of drill pipe connected end to end in a well while it is being drilled is called the drill string. The drill string connects the drill bit to the drilling rig. Rotating the drill string causes the bit to rotate.

Drilling Break - A sudden increase in the rate of penetration of the rock while drilling. A drilling break is experienced whenever the bit encounters a layer of rock that is easier to drill through. This can be a layer of rock with higher porosity and or higher pore pressure. If it is layer of higher porosity, then it may also be a pay zone; but a drilling break by itself does not mean that the bit has encountered a pay zone.

Drilling Rig - The equipment that is used to drill an oil and gas well. A rotary drilling rig consists of a hoisting system, a circulating system, and a rotary system. The hoisting system includes the substructure, derrick, crown block, traveling block, elevators, hook, and drawworks. The circulating system includes the mud pits or tanks, pumps, stand pipe, mud hose, swivel, drill string and shale shaker. The rotary system includes the kelly, kelly bushing, rotary table, drill pipe, drill collars, and drill bit. For more information about drilling rigs read the chapter about drilling a well.

Dry Gas - Gas that does not contain any significant amount of hydrocarbons that will condense in to a liquid phase if the pressure and or temperature of the gas are decreased. Dry gas is almost entirely composed of methane (CH_4).

Dual Completion - An arrangement of equipment within a wellbore that enables the well to produce oil and gas from two different pay zones simultaneously. The production from the pay zones are kept separate from one another by producing them through two different paths within the wellbore that are isolated from each other. Dual completions are more complex than single completions but they allow the

Operator to enjoy the time value of money benefit of producing two zones at the same time.

Estimated Ultimate Recovery - An estimate of the total amount of oil and gas that a well will produce over its entire lifetime from when it is drilled through the day that it is plugged and abandoned. The ultimate recovery of a well may be estimated by performing a decline curve analysis of the production history of the well and by analyzing the ultimate recoveries of nearby analogous wells. Multiplying the estimated ultimate recoveries of oil and gas by assumed product sales prices for each barrel of oil and each mcf of gas provides a potential investor with an estimate of the total revenue that a well will yield over its lifetime. For example, a shallow oil well that produces 50,000 barrels of oil over its lifetime of five years will yield gross revenue of $4,000,000 if the average price received for each barrel sold is $80. If that well can be drilled and evaluated for $250,000 and completed for an additional $250,000 it may represent an attractive investment for some investors.

Farm Out - An agreement where a party that holds the leasehold interest in an oil and gas lease (Lessee and Farmor) agrees to assign an interest in that Lease to another party (the Farmee) with the expectation that the Farmee will commence drilling operations on the lease and the Farmor will gain a benefit such as a retained interest in any successful wells that are drilled.

Fault - A fracture or crack through sedimentary rock where the rock layers on one side of the fracture have moved up, down, or sideways relative to the rock layers on the other side of the

164

fracture. During tectonic convergence, rocks may be compressed to the point that a fault forms and some rock layers are pushed up and over other rock layers that they were formerly beside. This kind of fault is called a reverse fault. The side of the fault where the rock layers have moved up relative to the other side is called the up-thrown side. The side of the fault where the rock layers have moved down relative to the other side is called the down-thrown side.

During tectonic extension or separation, rocks may be pulled apart in such a way that a fault forms and some rock layers slide down and away from the other rock layers that they were formerly beside. This kind of fault is called a normal fault. Normal faults form when continental plates are moving away from each other. The side of the fault where the rock layers have moved down relative to the other side is called the down-thrown side of the normal fault.

The higher side is called the up-thrown side.

Fee Ownership - In the oil and gas industry fee ownership usually means ownership of all interests in a property including mineral interests and surface rights. Hence, a fee interest owner may drill a well on their property without needing an oil and gas lease. There is a second and far less common meaning to the term "fee interest" in property law where "fee interest" means that the interest may be passed from one generation to another generation and thus indicates the potential duration of the interest rather than its composition.

FINRA - The Financial Industry Regulatory Authority (FINRA) is the largest independent regulator for all securities firms doing business in the United States. FINRA seeks to protect

America's investors by insuring that the securities industry operates fairly and honestly. FINRA oversees nearly 4,700 brokerage firms, about 167,000 branch offices, and approximately 637,000 registered securities representatives.

Fishing - An operation where an Operator is attempting to locate and retrieve any article that has been lost or left in a well. Such operations are known to be costly and time-consuming. A very wide range of tools are employed to latch on to items that are lost or left in a well. These are called fishing tools. The item an Operator is attempting to recover is called "the fish" regardless of what it is.

Folding - The bending of sedimentary rock layers in response to tectonic forces.

Formation - A layer of sedimentary rock. Its properties and characteristics are distinguishable from the layers of sedimentary rock above and below it.

Fracture - A crack in a formation. It may be natural or it may be the result of a hydraulic fracture stimulation. Unlike a fault, the rock on either side of the crack need not move relative to the rock on the other side for the opening to be considered a fracture.

Gamma Ray - Gamma rays are high-frequency short-wavelength electromagnetic radiation emitted from the nuclei of atoms. Gamma rays are continuously released in nature by certain isotopes of potassium, uranium, and thorium. One of the most common logging tools in the oil and gas industry is a gamma ray logging tool. A gamma ray tool counts the number of naturally emitted gamma rays produced by subsurface formations around the wellbore that are detected within a one-second time interval at the detector of the tool that is in the wellbore. Shales tend to contain more potassium than sandstones or carbonates. So higher gamma ray counts within a particular formation tend to indicate a higher percentage of shale. Formations with low gamma ray counts are called "clean" formations and these are most likely to be non-shales such as sandstones and carbonates. Gamma ray measurements are usually made every three to six inches for the entire length of a logged interval - which can be thousands of feet. Some gamma ray tools are capable of not only counting the number of gamma rays detected at the tool but also distinguishing the energy level of each gamma ray. This allows a Log Analyst to determine what elemental isotope emitted each gamma ray whether it was potassium, uranium, or thorium. These tools are called spectral gamma rays tools. Most gamma rays in most wells are emitted by potassium in shale. However, uranium and thorium sometimes appear in subsurface formations in high concentrations. Gamma rays emitted by uranium or thorium are not related to shale content and their presence can skew an analysis if their gamma rays are inadvertently assumed to be from shale. Gamma ray tools function in both open hole and cased hole. This fact allows cased hole tools such as perforating guns to be set in a well "on depth" with or "correlated" with specific zones seen on open hole logs that also included a gamma ray tool.

Gas - Also known as natural gas. A mixture of hydrocarbons that occur naturally in underground reservoirs in a gaseous phase or state. Natural gas composition is usually limited to varying amounts of methane (CH_4), ethane (C_2H_6), propane (C_3H_8), butane (C_4H_{10}), carbon dioxide (CO_2), oxygen (O_2), nitrogen (N_2), and hydrogen sulfide (H_2S). Though not all natural gases contain all of these molecules. Natural gas may also contain trace amounts of Helium, Neon, and Xenon. The term "dry gas" means a composition of natural gas that is almost entirely methane. "Wet gas" is a natural gas mixture that contains 80-90% methane with the remainder of the molecules including the natural gas liquids of ethane (C_2H_6), propane (C_3H_8), butane (C_4H_{10}) and some larger alkanes.

Gas Cap – A gas cap is an accumulation of gas above a zone of liquid oil or water in a porous layer of rock. A similar but much smaller gas cap can be found at the top of every bottle of soda before it is opened. If a gas cap exists above an oil zone, the Operator may initially attempt to produce only the oil and avoid producing gas from the gas cap so that the gas cap stays intact and pushes down on the oil for as long as possible and provides the pressure support that is necessary to recover as much oil as is possible. After the oil is produced, and there is no longer a need for the gas cap to push down on the oil, the gas in the gas cap can be produced.

Gas Cap Drive Oil Reservoir - In a gas cap drive oil reservoir, there is large gas reservoir immediately above and in communication with the oil reservoir. The pressure of the gas is exerted down against the oil. The pressure from the gas above the oil pressurizes the oil to equal the gas's pressure at the gas-oil interface. When the wellbore is perforated in the oil zone, the gas in the gas cap begins to push the oil toward the wellbore. If the wellbore perforations are made only in the oil zone and far below the gas cap, the initial production may at or near 100% oil. Over time some of the gas will begin to form a cone that extends down through the oil zone toward the perforations. Eventually some of this gas will "break-through" and be seen in the produced fluid along with the oil. From that point forward, the production will include both oil and gas. This is an undesirable circumstance because the production of gas from the gas cap will cause the pressure in the gas cap to decline and thus exert less press on the oil reservoir. As less pressure is exerted on the oil, the oil production rate decreases and the amount of oil that can ultimately be recovered is reduced. So when an Operator knows that an oil reservoir's drive mechanism is a gas cap, they will perforate wellbores only in the oil zone so that gas from the gas cap is not produced; and thus the pressure in the gas cap is kept as high as possible for as long as possible while oil is being produced.

Gas-Oil Ratio (GOR) - The ratio of produced gas to produced oil in a producing well measured in mcf of gas per barrel of oil.

Geologic Time Scale - The Earth is approximately 4.5 billion years old. Geologists have divided up that time in to smaller blocks of time and given those blocks of time names for ease of communication and called it the Geologic Time Scale. The largest blocks of time are Eons. Eons are divided in to Eras. Eras are further divided into Periods. Periods are divided in to Epochs. Epochs are divided into Ages. The most recent 542 million years of Earth's history are of the most interest to Petroleum Geologists because most life on Earth has lived during that time and it is in rocks of this Eon where most organic matter exists and where most oil and gas reservoirs are found. The diagram shows the Geologic Time Scale for the most recent 542 million years of Earth's history - an Eon known as the Phanerozoic Eon.

Geophone - A small device consisting of a coil of wire and a magnet hanging from a spring inside the coil of wire. Geophones are placed on the ground in seismic surveying operations to sense the movement of the ground up and down as compressional waves from the seismic source reflect off of layers of rock in the subsurface. As they travel back to the surface they cause an up and down oscillation of the ground. As the ground moves up and down, the coil inside the geophone moves up and down with the ground. But the magnet that is hanging from the spring does not move up and down as much as the coil of wire because it is hanging from a spring. So there is relative movement between the coil and the magnet as the ground moves up and down. This creates an alternating magnetic field around the magnet. As a result of the alternating magnetic field, the coil of wire outputs a small alternating voltage with a magnitude that varies directly with the velocity of the coil relative to the magnet. This alternating voltage of approximately 0.5 volts at its maximum is passed through amplifiers, noise filters, and analog to digital converters and recorded in a computer. The graphs of these output voltages of the geophones versus time constitute traces of seismic data.

Geophysicist - A Geophysicist is a person who uses their understanding of geophysical principles to study and describe the geology of the Earth. Geophysicists study seismic data to define prospective drilling locations.

Visit the Society of Exploration Geophysicists at www.seg.org

Gravity - Also known as API Gravity. A measure of the density of oil in degrees.

API Gravity = (141.5/Specific Gravity of the Oil at 60 degrees F) - 131.5

HBP - Held by Production. When a property is Held By Production, it means that the property is leased under the terms of an oil and gas lease and remains unavailable to be leased by other oil companies because at least one well on the property is producing oil and or gas.

Held By Production - Also known as HBP. When a property is Held By Production, it means that the property is leased under the terms of an oil and gas lease and remains unavailable to be leased by other oil companies because at least one well on the property is producing oil and or gas.

Horizontal Drilling - A form of directional drilling where an Operator intentionally and gradually deviates the trajectory of a well from vertical at the surface to horizontal at some deeper depth and then continues to drill horizontally - usually through a pay zone. An operator may drill a long section of the wellbore horizontally to maximize production rates and ultimate recovery by maximizing the surface area of the pay zone that is exposed to the wellbore; or with the intent to maximize the number of natural fractures in a pay zone that are penetrated by a wellbore. Many Operators drill horizontal wells in shale plays throughout the U.S.

Hydrocarbons - Organic compounds composed of the elements of hydrogen (H) and carbon (C). There are three major groups of hydrocarbons: alkanes, naphthenes, and aromatics.

The chemical formula of the first group of hydrocarbons, called alkanes, is C_nH_{2n+2} where n represents a varying number of carbon atoms in the molecules. Alkanes are chains of carbon atoms surrounded by hydrogen atoms. Common hydrocarbons that are of interest in the petroleum industry are the first eight members of the alkanes group: methane (CH_4), ethane (C_2H_6), propane (C_3H_8), butane (C_4H_{10}), pentane (C_5H_{12}), hexane (C_6H_{14}), heptane (C_7H_{16}), and octane (C_8H_{18}).

Alkane molecules with more than 20 carbon atoms are waxy solids at surface temperature and pressure. They are called paraffins.

Hydrocarbon molecules also form in rings with the chemical formula of

C_nH_{2n}. These are called naphthenes.

Benzene is a ring-shaped molecule that has the chemical formula of C_6H_6. To meet the valence requirements, a benzene ring includes three single bonds and three double bonds between the Carbon atoms. The benzene ring is the foundation of the group of hydrocarbons called aromatic hydrocarbons.

Initial Potential - Also known as the IP. The initial potential is the initial flow rate of oil or gas that a newly completed zone is determined to be capable of producing at as a result of a test. Newly completed zones are almost always tested soon after they are completed to determine their initial potential. The information obtained from the test is submitted to the state regulatory agency on a standard form. There is one form for oil wells and another form for gas wells.

Independent Oil Company - Any oil and gas exploration and production company that is not one of the major international oil companies and does not have refining operations. If you directly invest in an oil well, you will almost certainly be investing in a well that will be operated by an Independent Oil Company. For more information about independent oil companies, visit the Independent Petroleum Association of America at www.ipaa.org

Intangible Drilling Costs - Also known as IDC's. Intangible drilling costs are all of the costs of drilling and completing a well that do not include the purchase of any tangible item. Intangible drilling costs include all expenditures that have no salvage value. Casing, tubing, and surface production equipment may be salvageable after a well has finished producing and thus they are not included in intangible drilling costs.

The classification of every expenditure during the drilling and completion of a well as either intangible or tangible is important because federal tax law allows Operators and Investors to write off 100% of all intangible costs during the year that those expenses are incurred. Tangible costs must be capitalized and depreciated. Most of the costs of drilling and evaluating the productive capacity of a well are intangible drilling costs. Running production casing in a successful well is one of the first significant tangible costs.

Joint - Each individual section of drill pipe, casing, or tubing that is threaded on both ends is called a joint. Joints of drill pipe and joints of tubing are both approximately 30 feet long. Joints of casing are approximately 40 feet long. A drilling rig that is tall enough to pull two 30-foot joints of drill pipe (60 feet) at a time and stand them back in the derrick is called a "Double". A drilling rig that is tall enough to pull three 30-foot joints of drill pipe (90 ft) at a time and stand them back in the derrick is called a "Triple".

Joint Operating Agreement - Also known as a "J.O.A." A Joint Operating Agreement is a contract between the working interest owners of a petroleum property that describes how they will jointly develop and operate the property. It is an essential part of any direct oil and gas investment. There are two versions of JOA's that are widely used. They were promulgated by the American Association of Petroleum Land Men during the 1980's and they are still in use today. They are the A.A.P.L. Form 610-1982 Model Form Operating Agreement and the A.A.P.L. Form 610-1989 Model Form Operating Agreement. These documents were preceded by the A.A.P.L. 1956 Form and the A.A.P.L. 1977 Form.

Kelly and Kelly Bushing - A kelly (also known as a kelly joint) is special piece of pipe at the very top of the drill string that is square or hexagonal in cross-section. A kelly bushing is a device seated in the rotary table of the drilling rig that clenches the flat surfaces of the kelly and rotates the kelly. Rotating the kelly rotates the drill pipe below it and in turn rotates the drill bit. The kelly bushing turns the kelly similar to the way a wrench turns a nut. The kelly joint is free to move up and down through a hole in the kelly bushing. As the drill bit drills deeper the drill string moves down into the hole and the kelly moves down through the kelly bushing.

Land Man - A person who locates the owners of mineral interests in parcels of land and negotiates oil and gas leases for those parcels of land on behalf of an oil company. Land Men also work to cure defects in title. A Land Man may be male or female. Visit the American Association of Professional Land Men which has approximately 12,000 members at www. landman.org.

Lease - Also known as an oil and gas lease. An oil and gas lease is a written contract wherein a mineral interest owner, known as the Lessor, grants the right to explore for oil, natural gas, and other hydrocarbons to an oil company or other entity, known as the Lessee, for a specific period of time. An oil and gas lease is both a conveyance and a contract. It conveys certain mineral rights and establishes conditions which the Lessee must meet during the term of the lease. An oil and gas lease is considered a "Deed with the Possibility of Reverter" which means the interest may revert to the Lessor when the lease expires. For much more information see the chapter in this book about oil and gas leases.

Limestone - A sedimentary rock composed primarily of the mineral calcium carbonate. During the Paleozoic Era vast shallow seas covered much of North America and especially Texas. Marine life was abundant in these warm shallow seas. Shallow sea plants and animals including corals, echinoderms, anthozoans, bryozoans, algae, brachiopods, bivalves, cephalopods, gastropods, graptolites, and arthropods such as trilobites flourished in the warm waters. Some of these organisms such as corals and algae secreted calcium carbonate as part of their biologic processes during their life. Many of the other organisms retained calcium carbonate in their bodies, shells, and skeletons. Calcium carbonate sediments from both living and dead organisms built up on the sea floor over millions of years to form layers of limestone that are now thousands of feet thick. Many of these limestone formations hold millions of barrels of oil and billions of cubic feet of natural gas.

Logging - An operation where instruments with special sensors are lowered in to a well to measure certain electrical, physical, and nuclear properties of the rock strata surrounding the wellbore. The measurements are then analyzed to determine which formations contain commercial quantities of oil and gas and which do not. Logging tools can be conveyed in to and out of a wellbore on electric wireline or drill pipe. Some logging tools function only in open hole. Others function only in cased holes. The professionals who analyze log data are called Petrophysicists or Log Analysts. For more, visit the Society of

Petrophysicists and Well Log Analysts at www.spwla.org. They have local chapters throughout the world.

MCF - The most common unit of measurement of volume of natural gas in the United States. One MCF or mcf means one thousand cubic feet of natural gas at standard conditions of one atmosphere of pressure and 60 degrees Fahrenheit. Similarly, one MMCF or mmcf means 1,000 mcf or one million cubic feet of natural gas at standard conditions of one atmosphere of pressure and 60 degrees Fahrenheit.

Measured Depth - Abbreviated as MD, the measured depth of a well or a point in a well bore is the depth of that point from the surface as measured along the axis of the borehole. The true vertical depth of a well or a point in a wellbore is the depth as measured from that point directly to the surface along an imaginary vertical line that is perpendicular to the surface and extends through the point, regardless of whether or not the wellbore follows such a perfectly vertical line.

Measurement While Drilling (MWD) - A technology that an Operators uses to monitor and control the deviation and directional azimuth (compass direction) of a wellbore while it is being drilled. MWD tools have evolved to include LWD tools which means Logging While Drilling. In addition to monitoring deviation and azimuth while drilling, it is now possible to acquire log data such as gamma ray, resistivity, porosity, acoustics, and magnetic resonance measurements while drilling. These are LWD tools.

Mineral Interest - The right to explore for and produce oil, gas, and other minerals from a parcel of land. The mineral interest is conveyed from the mineral interest owner to the Lessee in an oil and gas lease.

Mother Hubbard Clause - A "Mother Hubbard" clause in an oil and gas lease is often included in the granting clause. It acts to include all land owned by the Lessor, if any, that are adjacent to and contiguous with the land in the legal description so that the lease covers all land owned by the Lessor in that location, regardless of whether the legal description perfectly describes the boundaries of the land. In this way, no small slivers of land are inadvertently left out of the lease.

Mud - Also known as drilling mud or drilling fluid. Mud is continuously circulated down the inside of the drill pipe, through the bit, and back up to the surface in the annulus while drilling operations are in progress. The serves several purposes. First, it provides a means of transporting the cuttings to the surface. Second, it provides the hydrostatic pressure that is necessary to offset the pore pressure of the fluids in the pores of the rock formations that the well is penetrating. If this hydrostatic pressure is not present or not sufficient, the well will blow out. And third, the mud cools and lubricates the drill bit as it turns. A Mud Engineer is an expert in the chemical and mechanical properties of drilling mud. A Mud Engineer may design a drilling fluid before a well is drilled and then frequently monitor the composition and properties of the actual drilling fluid while a well is being drilled. They can make adjustments as necessary. A Mud Report describing the composition and properties of the mud is usually produced at least once per day while a well is being drilled.

Mud Logger - This person analyzes cuttings recovered at the surface for lithology and the presence of oil, water, and gas. Some Mud Loggers also monitor the composition of the gas. Cuttings are small pieces of rock produced by the cutting action of a drill bit as it drills through a formation. Cuttings are cleared from the rock face beneath the drill bit and lifted to the surface by the circulation of drilling fluid down the inside to the drill pipe and back up the annulus. The annulus is the space between the borehole wall and the outside of the drill pipe. Cuttings are removed from the drilling fluid at the surface in a device called a shale shaker.

Natural Gas - A mixture of hydrocarbons that occurs naturally in underground reservoirs in a gaseous phase. Natural gas composition is usually limited to varying amounts of methane (CH_4), ethane (C_2H_6), propane (C_3H_8), butane (C_4H_{10}), carbon dioxide (CO_2), oxygen (O_2), nitrogen (N_2), and hydrogen sulfide (H_2S). Though not all natural gases contain all of these molecules. Natural gas may also contain trace amounts of Helium, Neon, and Xenon. The term "dry gas" means a composition of natural gas that is almost entirely methane. "Wet gas" is a natural gas mixture that contains 80-90% methane with the remainder of the molecules being the natural gas liquids of ethane (C_2H_6), propane (C_3H_8), butane (C_4H_{10}) and some larger alkanes.

Net Revenue Interest (NRI) - The net revenue interest is the revenue interest held in a petroleum property by the working interest owners after the burdens of mineral interest royalty and overriding royalties are subtracted.

For example, if an oil company leases a property with a 15% mineral interest royalty, and a 1% overriding royalty interest for the Land Man, then the Net Revenue Interest is 84%.

Normal Fault - A normal fault is a fault where the block of rock above the fault plane (the hanging wall) moves downward along the fault plane relative to the other block (the foot wall). A normal fault results from formations that are in tension. Normal faults are most likely to form when tectonic plates are moving apart or separating from one another.

Oil and Gas Lease - Also known simply as a lease. An oil and gas lease is a written contract wherein a mineral interest owner, known as the Lessor, grants the right to explore for oil, natural gas, and other hydrocarbons to an oil company or other entity, known as the Lessee, for a specific period of time. An oil and gas lease is both a conveyance and a contract. It conveys certain mineral rights and establishes conditions which the Lessee must meet during the term of the lease. An oil and gas lease is considered a "Deed with the Possibility of Reverter" which means the interest may revert to the Lessor when the lease expires. For much more information see the chapter in this book about oil and gas leases.

Open Hole - A section or interval of a wellbore where casing has not been run.

Operator - The working interest owner that is responsible for drilling, completion, production, workovers, lease management, accounting, and regulatory compliance for a petroleum property. The responsibilities of the

Operator are enumerated in the Joint Operating Agreement.

Outcrop - A place where an underground rock formation breaches the surface and is thus visible. Outcrops provide Geoscientists with rare opportunities to study rock formations that usually buried and thus impossible to see.

Overriding Royalty - Also known as an overriding royalty interest or ORRI or simply an override. An overriding royalty interest is a revenue interest in a petroleum property that is created by assignment from the working interest owner. Like a mineral interest owner's royalty, it entitles the owner to a percentage of the revenue from the property free of the costs of production but net of state taxes. An overriding royalty interest expires when the underlying oil and gas lease expires. Overriding royalty interests are often assigned by working interest owners to professionals such as Geologists, Geophysicists, Land Men, and Attorneys who contribute to the initial creation of an oil and gas project in lieu of or in addition to cash compensation.

Packer - A downhole tool that serves to block or plug the annulus either in cased hole or open hole.

Paid Up Lease - An oil and gas lease that does not have a provision for delay rentals. A paid-up lease is in effect from the day it is executed through the end of the primary term without the need for any delay rental payments.

Pay Zone - The sedimentary rock formation that contain commercial quantities of producible hydrocarbons.

Pay Out - The point in time in an oil and gas project when the working interest owners have recouped their initial exploration and development costs from the net proceeds of the sale of produced hydrocarbons.

Percentage Depletion - Depletion provides for the recovery of capital investment over time. Percentage depletion is a tax deduction that is calculated by applying an allowable percentage to the gross income from a property. For oil and natural gas the allowable percentage is 15 percent. This effectively means that 15% of a petroleum property's revenue from product sales is tax free. The law limits the use of the 15% percentage depletion deduction of oil and gas in several ways. First, the percentage depletion allowance may only be taken by independent producers and royalty owners and not by integrated oil companies. Second, depletion may only be claimed up to production levels of 1,000 barrels per day of oil or 6,000 mcf per day of natural gas. Third, the deduction is limited to 65% of net taxable income. Fourth, the net income limitation requires percentage depletion to be calculated on a property-by-property basis. It prohibits percentage depletion to the extent that it exceeds the net income from an individual property. These limitations apply both for regular and alternative minimum tax purposes. Percentage depletion in excess of the 65 percent limit may be carried over to future years until it is fully utilized.

Perforating - An operation where a device is lowered in to a well either on electric wireline or pipe and positioned within a pay zone and activated. The result is the creation of holes in the casing and the surrounding cement that extend in to the formation. Oil and gas can then flow from the formation, through the holes in the casing, and in to the well bore. There are a wide assortment perforating units in various shapes and sizes for various applications. The performances of the various units can be modeled prior to a perforating job to aid in selection.

Permeability - A measure of a rock's natural capacity to allow fluid to flow through it. Higher permeabilities are desirable because they allow for higher production rates and higher cumulative production if all other factors are constant. Permeability usually increases with increasing porosity. Increasing compaction, poorly sorted grains, and the presence of any form of cementation within the pore space all serve to decrease permeability. Approximations of permeability can be made using downhole formation testing tools and also with magnetic resonance devices.

Petroleum – Petroleum is a complex mixture of hydrocarbons. Hydrocarbons are molecules that are primarily composed of the chemical elements of Hydrogen (H) and Carbon (C). In nature, atoms of these two elements are combined in an infinite number of ways to create many different hydrocarbon molecules.

The simplest hydrocarbon molecule is methane. It contains a single carbon atom and four hydrogen atoms. Carbon has a valence of four and hydrogen has a valence of one. So hydrocarbon molecules tend to form structures that satisfy these valence numbers. All of the alkanes satisfy these requirements. The chemical formula of alkanes is C_nH_{2n+2} where n represents the number of carbon atoms in the molecule. Common hydrocarbons of the alkane group that are of interest in the petroleum industry are the first eight members of the alkanes group: methane (CH_4), ethane (C_2H_6), propane (C_3H_8), butane (C_4H_{10}), pentane (C_5H_{12}), hexane(C_5H_{14}), heptane (C_7H_{16}), and octane (C_8H_{18}). Alkane molecules with more than 20 carbon atoms are waxy solids at surface temperature and pressure. They are called paraffins. They can precipitate out of a liquid oil production stream in the wellbore and in surface equipment. Aside from alkanes, hydrocarbon molecules also form in rings with the chemical formula of C_nH_{2n}. These are called naphthenes. Benzene is another ring-shaped molecule that has the chemical formula of C_6H_6. A benzene ring includes three single bonds and three double bonds. Benzene forms the foundation of a group of hydrocarbons called aromatic hydrocarbons. Crude oil contains thousands of different molecules of alkanes, naphthenes, and aromatic hydrocarbons.

Petroleum is a complex mixture of hydrocarbons that may contain these and other hydrocarbons in varying compositions and proportions. The term "Petroleum" includes both liquid crude oil and natural gas and mixtures of the two. Crude oil composition varies. So its color, density, viscosity, and commercial value also vary. Crude oil can be clear, green, brown, yellowish, black, and all phases of color in between. The density varies from half of the density of water to denser than water. It can flow easily or resist flow with viscosities much like honey or tar. Its viscosity can also vary with temperature. Other compounds are sometimes mixed with the petroleum such as CO_2, H_2S, Nitrogen, and saline water. Petroleum that contains H_2S is dangerous because H_2S is a poisonous gas and it can be costly because it speeds the corrosion of metal equipment that it contacts such as casing and tubing. Crude oil that contains H_2S is referred to as sour crude. Alkanes can readily be separated from one another in a refinery and then sold in nearly pure form or used to create mixed products such as gasoline, diesel, and heating oil. For more information read the chapter about petroleum.

Petroleum Engineer - An Engineer who specializes in Oil and Gas Exploration and Production. Petroleum Engineering is further subdivided in to the three areas of Drilling, Production Engineering, and Reservoir Engineering. Many universities offer BS, MS, and PhD degrees in Petroleum Engineering. The Society of Petroleum Engineers (SPE) has tens of thousands of members worldwide.

Petroleum Geologist - A Geologist who specializes in oil and gas exploration and production. Many universities offer BS, MS, and PhD degrees in Petroleum Geology. The American Association of Petroleum Geologists (AAPG) has tens of thousands of members worldwide.

Plug and Abandon a Well - Also known as "Plugging and Abandoning" or P & A. This is the finally operation to permanently close a well. A well is permanently closed or abandoned for two primary reasons. First, when a new well is drilled and evaluated and found to be incapable of producing in paying quantities then it will be immediately plugged and abandoned. Such a well is known as a "Dry Hole". The "plugging" portion of the term "plug and abandon" refers to a part of the operation where cement is pumped into several sections of the wellbore to form permanent plus so that fluids will not be able to travel up or down inside the well after it is abandoned. The cost of plugging and abandoning a well must be included in the "Dry Hole Cost" of drilling a new well.

The second reason that a well is plugged and abandoned is that it has reached the end of its productive life and it is no longer capable of producing in paying quantities. All oil and gas wells are required to be plugged and abandoned when they are no longer capable of producing oil and gas.

Plugging and abandoning a well and involves removing any reusable downhole equipment from within the wellbore including tubing and casing.

The next step is to pump cement inside the wellbore at depths specified by the state regulatory agency. And finally the casing is cut off a few feet below ground level and a steel cap is welded on top of it. Then dirt is placed on top of it to make the ground level. If there are no other productive wells on the lease, the Operator will remove surface equipment and surface facilities. A plugging report is submitted by the Operator to the State Regulatory Agency at the time a well is plugged and these reports are available to the public.

Plug Back - To block a deeper section of a wellbore where an Operator has been producing from and move up the hole to initiate production in a shallower pay zone. Plugging back is a permanent abandonment of the deeper zone.

Pooling - Combining adjacent tracts of land that are under different oil and gas leases to assemble enough contiguous acreage to meet the minimum drilling spacing unit required by the state regulatory agency to obtain a drilling permit. Some oil and gas leases grant the Lessee the right but not the obligation to pool all or any part of the leased premises with any other lands whenever the Lessee deems it necessary.

Porosity - The ratio of pore space within a rock to the total volume of the rock. Porosities of oil and gas reservoirs typically range from 5% to 35%. Higher porosities are better than low porosities because higher porosities mean there is more space occupied by oil and gas.

Primary Term - The primary term is the period of time designated in the habendum clause in most oil and gas leases during which an Operator is granted the right to begin drilling operations without the obligation to do so. Most oil and gas leases state that the lease shall be in force for a primary term of a specific number of years -- typically one to five years -- from the date that the lease is executed, and for as long thereafter as oil or gas or other substances are produced in paying quantities from the leased premises or from lands pooled or unitized therewith. If the lease is not producing in paying quantities and the Operator is not engaged in continuous drilling operations at the end of the primary term, then the oil and gas lease terminates.

Prospect - A geographic area where one or more people believe that commercial quantities of oil and gas may exist underground. The area may be large or small and may be tested by a single well or it can require many wells for appraisal and development. A prospect is a drilling idea that can be bought and sold with or without an oil and gas lease existing at the location.

Re-Entry - The operation of opening and entering a wellbore that was previously plugged and abandoned in an effort to restore production in a zone that was previously producing - or - initiate production in a zone that had not previously been produced -or- to deepen the well to produce hydrocarbons from a zone that is deeper than the total depth of the well.

Reserves - The amount of oil or gas available to be produced from one or more reservoirs.

Reservoir - A body of porous and permeable rock where hydrocarbons accumulate in commercial quantities and are produced from.

Resistivity - A property of a material that describes its resistance to the flow of electricity. Resistivity is one of the primary logging measurements made in oil and gas wells. Resistivity logs can be run on electric wireline or on drill pipe. With the exception of some clays, grains of rock do not conduct electricity. And oil and gas do not conduct electricity. Saline formation water does conduct electricity. So generally speaking, if the salinity of formation water is constant, then the resistivity of a formation is inversely related to porosity. However, if a formation is logged with high porosity and high resistivity, the high resistivity may be indicative of that formation being saturated with oil and gas rather than saline water. The unit of measurement of resistivity is ohm-meters. The inverse of resistivity is conductivity.

Reverse Fault - A reverse fault is a fault where the block of rock above the fault plane (the hanging wall) moves upward along the fault plane relative to the other block (the foot wall). A reverse fault occurs when formations are in compression. Reverse faults are most likely to form when tectonic plates are converging.

Reversionary Interest - An interest in a petroleum property that becomes effective at a contractually specified date or when certain contractually specified conditions are met.

Risk - The possibility of loss associated with an uncertainty. Every investment in the oil and gas industry has risk.

Roughneck - A person who works on a drilling rig during drilling operations. A crew of roughnecks is lead by a Driller who controls the hoisting system, rotary system, and pumping system on a drilling rig. Drillers and roughnecks are supervised by a Tool Pusher who is the highest ranking person working for the drilling contractor at a drilling location.

Royalty - A share of the proceeds from the sale of oil and gas produced from a petroleum property apart from that of the working interest owners. Royalties include mineral interest owner's royalty which is paid to the land owner or mineral interest owner and overriding royalty which is assigned by working interest owners to professionals such as Geologists, Geophysicists, Land Men, and Attorneys who contribute to the initial creation of an oil and gas project in lieu of or in addition to cash compensation.

Sandstone - A sedimentary rock formed by the cementing together and lithification of quartz grains. Quartz grains are composed of mineral silica which has the chemical formula of SiO_2. Sandstone is a clastic sedimentary rock which means it consists of individual fragments called clasts that were produced by the weathering of previous rock formations. Sandstone is a common reservoir rock for oil and gas.

Saturation - The percentage of the pore space within a formation that is occupied by a particular fluid. Oil saturation (So) is the percentage of the pore space within a formation that is occupied by oil. Gas saturation (Sg) is the percentage of the pore space within a formation that is occupied by gas. Water saturation (Sw) is the percentage of the pore space within a formation that is occupied by water. A formation that contains nothing but water has a water saturation of 100%. The sum of Oil Saturation plus Gas Saturation plus Water Saturation is 100%.

Secondary Term – The secondary term is the period of time when an oil and gas lease remains in effect after the primary term. The primary term of an oil and gas lease is the period of time in most oil and gas leases that an Operator is granted to begin drilling operations or lose the lease for failure to do so. Most oil and gas leases state that the lease shall be in force for a primary term of a specific number of years -- typically one to five years - from the date that the lease is executed, and for as long thereafter as oil or gas or other substances are produced in paying quantities. If the lease is not producing in paying quantities and the Operator is not engaged in continuous drilling operations at the end of the primary term, then the oil and gas lease terminates. But if the lease is producing oil or gas in paying quantities after the primary term or the Operator is conducting continuous drilling operations after the primary term, the lease remains in effect. This period of time when the lease remains in effect after the primary term is the secondary term.

Section - A square mile of land. 640 acres in the shape of a square.

Securities Act of 1933 - Often referred to as the "Truth in Securities" Law, the Securities Act of 1933 has two basic objectives: To require that investors receive financial and other significant information concerning securities being offered for public sale; and to prohibit deceit, misrepresentations, and other fraud in the sale of securities. The primary means of accomplishing these goals is the disclosure of important financial information through the registering of securities. This information enables investors, not the government, to make informed judgments about whether or not to purchase a company's securities.

In general, the registration forms require

(1) a description of the company's properties and business; (2) a description of the security to be offered for sale; (3) information about the management of the company; and (4) financial statements certified by independent Accountants.

Not all offerings of securities must be registered with the Securities and Exchange Commission. Some exemptions from the requirements exist for (1) private offerings to a limited number of persons or institutions; (2) offerings of limited size; (3) intrastate offerings; and (4) securities of municipal, state, and federal governments. By exempting many small offerings from the registration process, the government seeks to foster capital formation by lowering the cost of offering securities to the public.

Securities Act of 1934 - This Act created the Securities and Exchange Commission and grants it broad authority over all aspects of the securities industry. This includes the power to register, regulate, and oversee brokerage firms, transfer agents, and clearing agencies as well as the nation's self regulatory organizations such as FINRA.

Security - A "security" includes any [limited partner interest in a limited partnership, share, stock, treasury stock, stock certificate under a voting trust agreement, collateral trust certificate, equipment trust certificate, preorganization certificate or receipt, subscription or reorganization certificate, note, bond, debenture, mortgage certificate or other evidence of indebtedness, any form of commercial paper, certificate] **in or under a** [profit sharing or participation agreement, certificate or any instrument representing any interest in or under an oil, gas, or mining lease, fee or title, or any certificate or instrument representing or secured by an interest in any or all of the capital, property, assets, profits or earnings of any company, investment contract, or any other instrument commonly known as a security], whether similar to those herein referred to or not and regardless of whether the "security" or "securities" are evidenced by a written instrument. For more information about the regulation of securities, visit the U.S. Securities and Exchange Commission and the State Securities Boards in the state where your prospective projects are located.

Sedimentary Rocks - Sedimentary rocks are one of three classes of rocks: igneous, sedimentary, and metamorphic. Sedimentary rocks are formed when older rocks are broken down by weathering or biogenic processes, then transported by water, wind, or ice, and finally deposited in layers of sediment. These layers of sediment are later compacted by the weight of further sediment above them. They later harden, or lithify, to form continuous solid rock. Sedimentary rocks may contain a wide array of minerals but the most common minerals are quartz, feldspar, clays, calcite, dolomite, and evaporites. Sedimentary rocks can be divided in to three types: Carbonates, Clastics, and Precipitates.

Carbonate sedimentary rocks are composed of limestone which is the mineral calcite ($Ca\ CO_3$). In some cases magnesium enters the rock and replaces half of the calcium and thus changes the calcite to dolomite ($Ca\ Mg\ (CO_3)_2$). Carbonate sedimentary rocks are formed from the deposition of the remains of marine organisms or from calcium carbonate produced by the biologic processes of living organisms in shallow or deep seas. These organisms include algae, shells, and single-cell organisms.

Clastic sedimentary rocks are separated in to four groups based on grain size. They are conglomerates, sandstone, siltstone, and mudstone or shale. Shale is a general description for a rock that is deposited in a low energy environment and is composed of varying amounts of hydrous aluminosilicate clays such as kaolinite, illite, and smectite, together with fine-grain silica (silts), calcite, and sometimes organic material known as kerogen. Shales are often found interbedded or mixed with sandstone. Clean sandstone is a term that describes sandstone without shale.

Precipitates, or chemical sedimentary rocks, form when material precipitates from solution and later lithifys into solid rock. The most common examples are evaporates such as salt and gypsum which form in vast thick layers when the water in a sea evaporates.

Most of the oil and gas in the world has been produced from sedimentary rocks. The sedimentary rocks that hold oil and natural gas are usually limestone, dolomite, sandstone, or shale or mixtures of these.

Seismic Surveying - An operation where compressional waves from an energy source on the surface are sent down in to the Earth's subsurface. Those compressional waves reflect off of the surfaces of underground formations. Technically speaking there is a reflection any time a compressional wave reaches a point where there is a change in acoustic impedance. When the reflected waves reach the surface the ground moves up and down in very small increments. The ground movements caused by the arrival of the reflected waves are detected by geophones and the output voltages of the geophones are recorded on computers. The plots of output voltages from the geophones versus time are later interpreted to determine the structures of subsurface formations and in some cases obtain clues as to the nature of the fluid in the pores of those formations - be they liquid or gas. The energy source on the surface can be a vibroseis truck, an air gun submerged in a pit of water, or dynamite buried approximately 100 feet underground. Vibroseis trucks (also known as vibe trucks) use a very heavy vibrating plate that vibrates against the ground. The vibrations are controlled by the truck. They typically perform a "sweep" of vibrations from a low frequency to a high frequency lasting about 8-10 seconds.

Separator - A piece of surface production equipment that separates the oil, gas, and water in a production stream.

Severance Tax - A tax paid on the proceeds of produced oil and gas to state and county taxing jurisdictions. Royalty owners are usually responsible for paying the severance taxes on their share of the proceeds from production.

Shale - A general description of a clastic sedimentary rock that is deposited in a low energy environment and is composed of varying amounts of hydrous aluminosilicate clays such as kaolinite, illite, and smectite, together with fine-grain silica (silts), sometimes some calcite, and in some cases organic material known as kerogen. Shales are often found interbedded or mixed with sandstone. Clean sandstone is a term that describes sandstone without shale. Shale can produce oil and gas. The most prominent shale plays in the United States are the Barnett Shale in north Texas, the Haynesville Shale in east Texas and north Louisiana, the Woodford Shale in Oklahoma, the Eagle Ford Shale in south Texas, the Fayetteville Shale in Arkansas, the Bakken Shale in North Dakota, and the Marcellus Shale in the Northeast.

Shale Shaker - Also known simply as a "shaker". This is a device on a drilling rig that is used to separate cuttings from the drilling fluid as the drilling fluid returns to the surface during drilling operations.

Show - A show is almost anything that is seen during the drilling of a well or on a log that makes someone think there might be oil and gas in a particular zone. A "show" is often seen on a mud log or a wireline log. A show alerts an Operator to pay closer attention to a particular zone. Anyone can declare almost anything to be a show. There is nothing conclusive about seeing or having a "show".

Shut-In a Well - To take the physical actions necessary to cause a well to stop producing. It can be as simple as closing a valve.

Shut-In Royalty - A special kind of royalty provided in an oil and gas lease that states that if after the primary term one or more wells on the leased premises or lands pooled or unitized therewith are capable of producing oil and gas in paying quantities, but the well or wells are either shut in or production therefrom is not being sold by the Operator, then the Operator will pay a shut-in royalty to the Lessor of a certain number of dollars per acre as specified in the Lease.

Sidetrack - A wellbore that branches off of a previously drilled wellbore. Sidetracks are almost never planned prior to spudding a well. They are contingencies that are drilled when the first wellbore either becomes unusable (as a result of equipment being lost in the hole or circulation problems) or does not intersect the desired formation in the desired location. The tool that used to initiate a sidetrack by diverting a drill bit in to the side of an existing wellbore is called a whipstock.

Solution Gas Drive Oil Reservoir - In a solution gas drive reservoir, there is hydrocarbon gas dissolved inside the liquid oil in a reservoir. As oil is produced the pressure of the reservoir declines an some of the dissolved gas comes out of solution and forms small bubbles of gas inside the pore of the reservoir rock. The pressure from these bubbles pushes the oil toward the wellbore. The gas-oil ratio will increase with time. With all other things being equal, a solution gas drive oil reservoir will yield an ultimate oil recovery that is less than a Water Drive Oil Reservoir.

Sour Crude Oil - Also known as "sour crude". Sour crude oil is crude oil that contains significant amounts of hydrogen sulfide (H_2S). "Sweet crude" does not have hydrogen sulfide. Sweet crude is preferable to sour crude because it costs less to refine.

Sour Gas - Sour gas is natural gas that contains significant amounts of hydrogen sulfide (H_2S).

Source Rock - A sedimentary rock formation that contains organic material. When the formation is buried under younger sediments and compressed and heated, some of the organic material is converted to oil and gas which later migrates up though the formations above the source rock until it is trapped below an impermeable layer of rock and accumulates to form a reservoir. Shales are often the source rocks for limestone and sandstone reservoirs that lay above them. Shales can be both source rocks and producing reservoirs.

Spud - To begin drilling a well. Drilling the very first inch of depth in a well is spudding the well.

Stripper Well - A well that produces less than 15 barrels of oil per day.

Surface Rights - Mineral rights can be severed from surface rights in a property. The surface rights are all rights in a parcel of land except the mineral interest. Surface rights are servient to the mineral rights. The surface interest enjoys the right to the surface subject to the mineral interest.

Sweet Crude Oil - Also known as "sweet crude". Sweet crude oil is crude oil that does not contain significant amounts of hydrogen sulfide (H_2S). Sweet crude is preferable to sour crude because it costs less to refine.

Tank Battery - A group of tanks in a single location. A tank battery usually includes oil stock tanks and may include a gun barrel and a water tank. Tanker trucks visit tank batteries regularly to load the crude oil that is in the oil stock tanks and haul it to pipeline injection points. Tanker trucks also visit tank batteries regularly to load the water that is stored in the water tanks and haul it away to a disposal well.

TD - Total Depth. The maximum depth of a well.

Tight Formation - A formation that has relatively low permeability.

Tool Pusher - also known simply as the "Pusher". The Tool Pusher is the highest ranking person working for the drilling contractor at a drilling location. A crew of roughnecks is lead by a Driller who controls the hoisting system, rotary system, and pumping system on a drilling rig. Drillers and roughnecks are supervised by the Tool Pusher. Tool Pushers have many years of previous experience as Roughnecks and Drillers.

Trap - A natural seal in underground layers of sedimentary rock that prohibits hydrocarbons from migrating vertically through it. When migrating hydrocarbons accumulate under a trap a reservoir is formed.

Trip - A trip is the movement of all of the drill pipe or tubing either into or out of a well. "Tripping Out" means pulling all of the drill pipe or tubing out of a well. "Tripping In" means running all of the drill pipe or tubing that is on surface in to a well. Tripping may be performed during drilling operation to change the drill bit if it has become excessively worn. Tripping may be performed during a workover to replace a joint of tubing that has developed a hole in it.

True Vertical Depth - Abbreviated as TVD, the true vertical depth of a well or a point in a wellbore as measured from that point directly to the surface along an imaginary vertical line that is perpendicular to the surface and extends through the point, regardless of whether or not the wellbore follows such a perfectly vertical line. The "measured depth" of a well or a point in the well bore, abbreviated as MD, is the depth from the surface as measured along the path of the borehole.

Tubing - Small diameter pipe that is lowered in to a cased well that provides a conduit for oil and gas to be produced through. In the United States, tubing is commonly 2-3/8 inches or 2-7/8 inches in diameter.

Turnkey - A contractual arrangement where a drilling contractor agrees to drill a well to an agreed total depth with agreed specifications for a fixed price and the Operator is not liable for payment of the fixed price to the drilling contractor unless and until a well is successfully drilled to the agreed total depth and meets the other agreed specifications. A turnkey contract places most of the operational risk of successfully drilling a well on the drilling contractor. If there are unforeseen problems during the drilling operation, the Operator is protected by having a Turnkey contract which limits their drilling cost.

Undivided Interest – An ownership interest where a party owns an interest in a property with one or more other parties and their interests are not separated in to separate parcels with separate legal descriptions. Each party owns a percentage of the same property which has only one legal description.

Viscosity - A measure of a fluid's resistance to flow. Oilfield units for viscosity are centipoise (cp). A centipoise is one one-hundredth of a poise. A poise is one gram/centimeter/second.

Volumetric Gas Reservoir - In a volumetric gas reservoir, gas exists by itself within the pores of the rock without any oil or water at the reservoir boundaries and within a relatively fixed volume. The pressure of the gas simply declines as the gas is produced. Producing a volumetric gas reservoir (also known as a depletion drive gas reservoir) is similar to opening the valve on a scuba diver's air tank and allowing the air to blow out. The most efficient drive mechanism for producing gas is a volumetric reservoir. It provides the highest ultimate recovery.

Water Drive Gas Reservoir - In a water drive gas reservoir, there is a large water reservoir below the gas reservoir and it pushes against the gas and displaces the gas like a piston as the gas is produced. If the wellbore perforations are only in the gas zone and completely above the water, the initial production may at or near 100% gas. Because the water moves up and displaces gas as the gas is produced, the gas reservoir's pressure may not decline significantly. If the permeability is high then the reservoir pressure and the gas flow rate will be nearly constant over time. From the Operator's viewpoint, the well seems as if it will produce at a constant rate indefinitely. This characteristic can make the well appear to be an attractive purchase. However, as soon as the water that is displacing the gas from below reaches the perforations in the wellbore, the gas production will suddenly cease.

Some Operators produce water drive gas reservoirs at very high rates in the

236

hope that they can produce gas from locations in the reservoir that are both above and below the perforations. Others choose to produce these reservoirs at very slow rates so as to minimize the pressure differential between the water and the perforations and thus minimize the odds of "coning" water up to the perforations from the water below. The downside of this method is that any gas that is in the reservoir but above the depth of the perforations will not be produced and will be left in the reservoir at full reservoir pressure. Water drive gas reservoirs have a relatively constant flowing tubing pressure and flow rate until the day when the water reaches the perforations and all gas production suddenly ceases.

Water Drive Oil Reservoir - In a water drive oil reservoir, there is a large water reservoir below the oil reservoir and it pushes against the oil and displaces it like a piston. The pressure from the water below acts on the oil and pressurizes it to equal the water's pressure at the oil-water interface. When the wellbore is perforated, the water begins to push the oil toward the wellbore. If the wellbore perforations are only in the oil zone and completely above the water, the initial production may be at or near 100% oil. Over time some of the water will begin to "finger through" in homogeneities of the oil zone where the relative permeability of water is higher. Eventually some of this water will "break-through" and be seen in the produced fluid along with the oil. From that point forward, the production will include both oil and water. The production rate of oil will decline exponentially over time.

Roughly 80% of all wells have a production decline rate that is between 12% and 30%. A 12% exponential decline rate means that each year a well produces 88% of the amount of oil that it produced in the preceding year. A 30% exponential decline rate means that each year a well produces 70% of the amount of oil that it produced in the preceding year. All other things being equal, an oil reservoir with a water-drive mechanism will have a lower (better) decline rate and a higher ultimate recovery than an equivalent reservoir with any other drive mechanism. Water-drive is the most efficient drive mechanism for producing oil.

Water-Wet - A condition where the interfacial tension between the grains of rock in a formation and the formation water is less than the interfacial tension between the grains of the rock and oil in the formation. A water-wet reservoir is preferable to an oil-wet reservoir when initiating a water flood.

Wet - A wet formation is a formation with pore space that is 100% saturated with water. Oil and gas cannot be produced from wet zones because wet zones do not contain oil or gas. Porous wet zones containing saline formation water tend to have relatively low resistivity.

Wildcat - A well that is drilled far from any previously drilled wells.

Working Interest - The Lessee's interest in a petroleum property that is created when an oil and gas lease is executed. The working interest is entitled to all revenues from production after subtracting the mineral interest owner's royalty and any overriding royalty interests that the working interest owner has assigned.

Oil and Gas Web Sites

State Oil and Gas Regulatory Agencies

Alabama

http://www.gsa.state.al.us/

California

http://www.conservation.ca.gov/

Colorado

http://cogcc.state.co.us/

Florida

http://www.dep.state.fl.us/water/
mines/oil_gas/index.htm

Illinois

http://dnr.state.il.us/mines/dog/

Indiana

http://www.in.gov/dnr/

Kansas

http://www.kcc.state.ks.us/
conservation/index.htm

Kentucky

http://oilandgas.ky.gov/

Louisiana

http://dnr.louisiana.gov/min/

Mississippi

http://www.ogb.state.ms.us/

Montana

http://bogc.dnrc.state.mt.us/

Nevada

http://minerals.state.nv.us/

New Mexico

http://www.emnrd.state.nm.us/ocd/

New York

http://www.dec.ny.gov/about/805.
html

North Dakota

https://www.dmr.nd.gov/oilgas/

Oklahoma

http://www.occeweb.com

Pennsylvania

http://www.dep.state.pa.us/dep/
deputate/minres/oilgas/oilgas.htm

Texas

http://www.rrc.state.tx.us/

Wyoming

http://wogcc.state.wy.us/

Government Web Sites

U.S. Energy Information Administration
http://www.eia.doe.gov/

U.S. Energy Information Administration
Annual Energy Outlook http://www.
eia.doe.gov/oiaf/aeo/

U.S. Geological Survey National Oil
andGas Assessment http://energy.
cr.usgs.gov/oilgas/noga/

SEC Reg D Offerings http://www.sec.
gov/answers/regd.htm

Publications

American Oil and Gas Reporter

http://www.aogr.com/

Oil and Gas Investor

http://www.oilandgasinvestor.com/

Rig Zone

http://www.rigzone.com/

Organizations

American Petroleum Institute
http://www.api.org/

Independent Petroleum Association of
America http://www.ipaa.org/

American Association of Professional
Land Men http://www.ipaa.org/

Society of Petroleum Engineers http://
www.spe.org

American Association of Petroleum
Geologists http://www.aapg.org/

Society of Exploration Geophysicists

http://www.seg.org/

Bureau of Economic Geology

http://www.beg.utexas.edu

Oil and Gas Prices

CME Futures Contract Quotes

http://www.cmegroup.com/trading/energy/

Oil and Gas Trade Shows

NAPE - North American Prospect Expo

http://www.napeexpo.com/

PBIOS - Permian Basin International Oil Show

http://www.pbioilshow.org/

PLS – PLS Dealmakers Expos

http://www.plsx.com/

Public

Bureau of Economic Geology
http://www.beg.utexas.edu

North Dakota Oil and Gas Leasing Considerations
https://www.dmr.nd.gov/oilgas/
leasingconsiderations.pdf

Weiss Energy Hall at the Houston Museum of Natural Science http://www.hmns.org

Permian Basin Petroleum Museum
http://www.petroleummuseum.org

About the Author

Mike May is a Licensed Professional Petroleum Engineer. He has over 20 years of experience in the oil and gas industry. His geographic experience includes oil and gas wells located in Texas, Louisiana, California, North Dakota, Washington, Wyoming, the Gulf of Mexico, Trinidad, Argentina, the United Kingdom, Romania, Azerbaijan, North Africa, Iraq, India, Vietnam, and Malaysia.

He has advised ExxonMobil, Shell, Apache, Conoco, Statoil Hydro, Newfield Exploration, Nexen Petroleum, Cairn Energy, Reliance Industries of India, and more than 50 smaller independent oil companies.

Mike has spoken to oil and gas industry audiences around the world from oil companies in Houston to the Geological Society of London to technology seminars in India. He has spoken about a wide range of advanced downhole technologies including formation fluid sampling and pressure testing.

Mike specializes in formation evaluation and while representing one of the big three service companies he was responsible for all electric wireline operations for a major international oil company with operations in 15 countries. Prior to that he performed over 700 open hole logging jobs in the field, analyzed thousands of formations, and helped clients assess the commercial viability of hundreds of wells by analyzing open hole logs at the casing point.

Mike is an expert in the computer modeling of downhole perforation performance. He has designed numerous perforating jobs from Texas to Iraq.

He has been the lead negotiator of several oilfield service contracts with a total value in nine figures.

Mike has experience in Petrophysics, Log Analysis, Downhole Formation Fluid Testing and Sampling, Electric Wireline

Operations, Petroleum Geology, Reservoir Engineering, Drilling, Completions, Seismic and Geophysics.

Mike lives in Houston, Texas. He is the owner of Limestone Oil.

He leases land and creates oil and gas drilling projects in the United States.

Mike May, P.E.

(832) 382-9976

Mike.May @ Limestone Oil .com

www. Negotiating Oil and Gas Leases .com

15042725R00144

Made in the USA
Lexington, KY
04 May 2012